THE MOST REQUE[illegible]
Christmas Songs

Cherry Lane Music Company
Director of Publications/Project Editor: Mark Phillips

ISBN 978-1-4584-1274-4

Visit our website at www.cherrylaneprint.com

CONTENTS

All I Want for Christmas Is You

Words and Music by
Mariah Carey and Walter Afanasieff

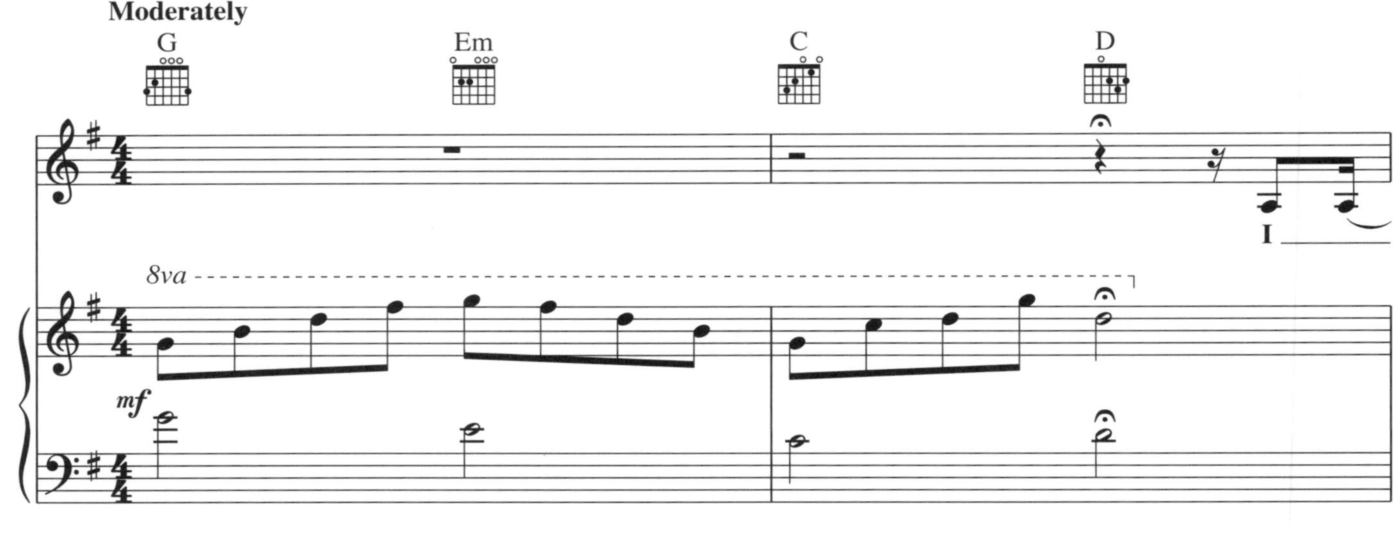

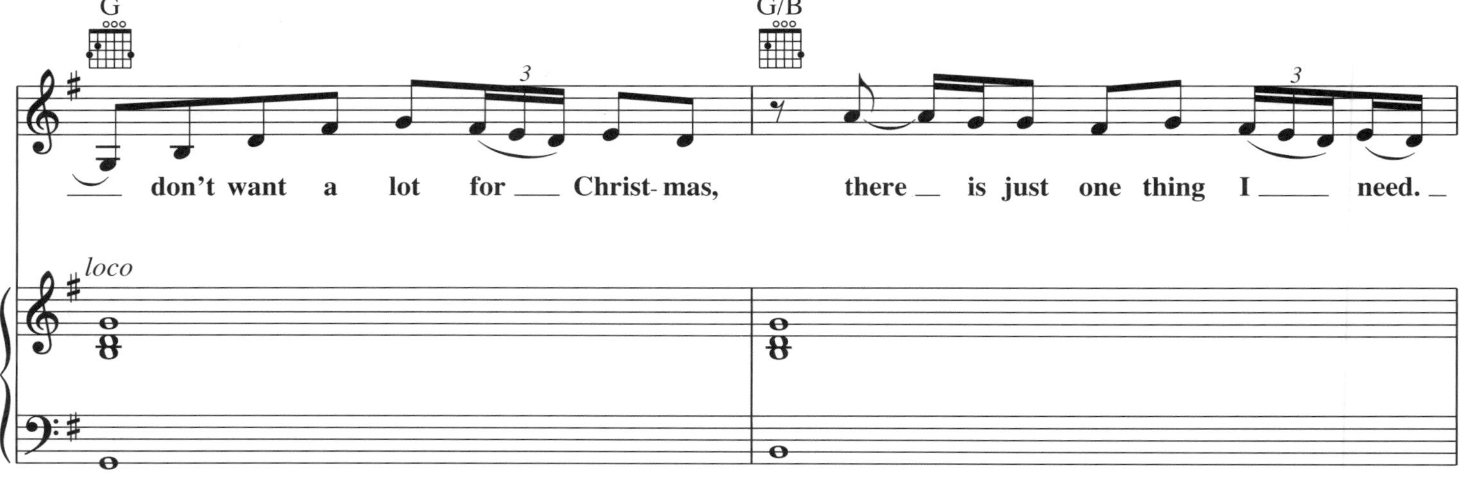

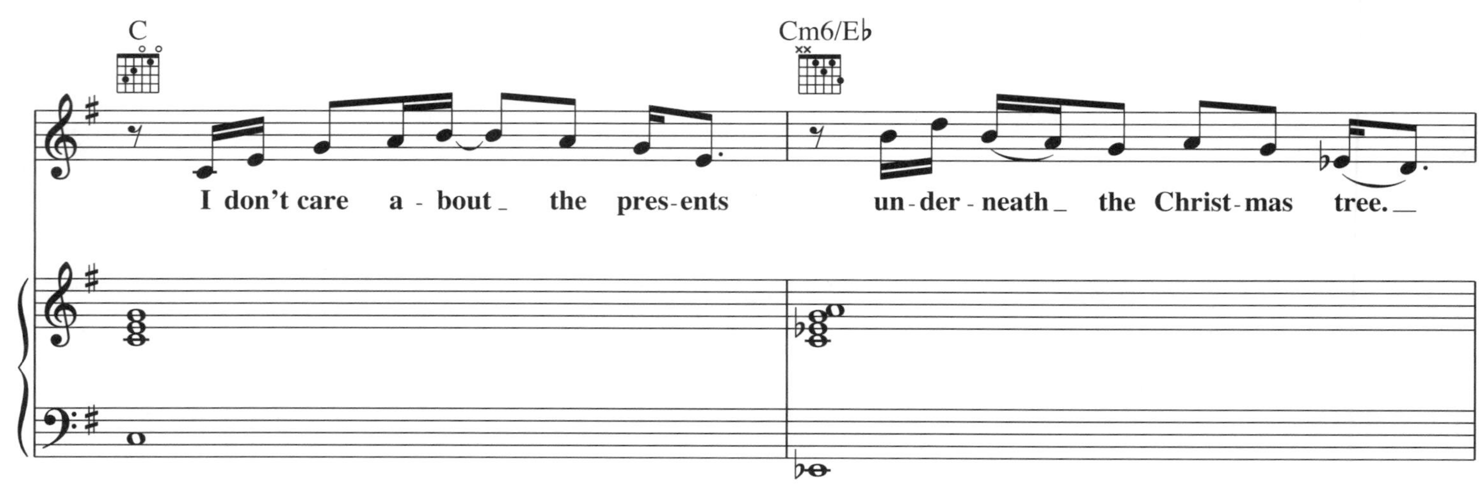

G/D
B7♯5
Em
Cm6/E♭
I just want you for my own, more than you could ev - er know.
G/D
E7
Am7
Am7♭5/D
3fr
Make my wish come true: all I want for Christ-mas is you,
G
Moderately fast
Em
C
D
yeah.

G
I don't want a lot for Christ-mas, there is just one thing
I won't ask for much this Christ-mas, I won't e-ven wish
C
I need And I don't care a-bout the pres-ents,
for snow. And I, I'm just gon-na keep on wait-ing
Cm6/E♭
un-der-neath the Christ-mas tree.
un-der-neath the mis-tle-toe.
G
I don't need to hang my stock-ing there up-on the fi-
I won't make a list and send it to the North Pole for
I don't want a lot for Christ-mas, this is all I'm ask-

C
- re - place.
Santa Claus won't make me happy
Saint Nick.
I won't e - ven stay a - wake to
- ing for.
I just want to see my ba - by
Cm6/E♭
with a toy on Christ - mas day
hear those mag - ic rein - deer click.
stand - ing right out - side my door.
G
B7
Em
I just want you for my own,
more than you could ev -
I just want you here to - night,
hold - ing on to me
I just want him for my own,
more than you could ev -
Cm6/E♭
G/D
- er know.
Make my wish come true:
so tight.
What more can I do?
- er know.
Make my wish come true:

E7
Am9
To Coda
Am7♭5/D
3 fr
all I want for Christ - mas is
Ba - by all I want for Christ - mas is
G
Em
Am9
you.
you.
You,
You,
3
1
D7
2
D7
B7
ba - by. Oh,
ba - by. Oh,
All the lights
Em
are shin - ing so bright - ly ev - 'ry - where,

B7
Em
and the sound of chil - dren's laugh - ter fills the air,
Cm6/E♭
And ev - 'ry - one is sing - ing.
G/D
E7
Am9
I hear those sleigh bells ring - ing. San - ta won't you please bring me
D7
D.S. al Coda
what I real - ly need, won't you please bring my ba - by to me. Oh,

CODA
Am7
Am7♭5/D
3 fr
all I want for Christ - mas
G
Em
is
you.
Am9
D7
G
Ooh,
ba - by.
All I want for
Em
Am9
D7
Repeat and Fade
Christ - mas is you,
ba - by.

Baby, It's Cold Outside

from the Motion Picture NEPTUNE'S DAUGHTER

By Frank Loesser

Bb6
Cm7
Bb/D
Gm7
Gb9
3fr
eve - ning has been so ver - y
wel - come has been so nice and
Been hop - ing that you'd drop in.
How luck - y that you dropped in.
Fm9
Bb9#11
Fm9
Bb13
6fr
E9
Ebmaj9
Eb6/9
5fr
nice. My moth - er will start to
warm. My sis - ter will be sus -
I'll hold your hands. They're just like ice.
Look out the win - dow at the storm.
Ebmaj9
Eb6/9
5fr
Ebm7/Ab
6fr
Ab9
4fr
wor - ry, and Fa - ther will be pac - ing the
pi - cious. My broth - er will be there at the
Beau - ti - ful, what's your hur - ry?
Gosh, your lips look de - li - cious. Like

E♭m7/A♭
A♭7
B♭9♯11
A♭13♯11
floor. So real - ly, ha! I'd bet - ter scur -
door. My maid - en aunt's mind is
Lis - ten to the fi - re - place roar.
waves up - on a trop - i - cal shore.
G7♯9
D♭9♯11
C13
C7♭13
Cm7/F
ry! Well, may - be just a half a drink more. My
vi - cious. Well, may - be just a cig - a - rette more. I've
Beau - ti - ful, please don't hur - ry. Put some rec - ords on while I pour.
Gosh, your lips are de - li - cious. Nev - er such a bliz zard be - fore.
B♭6
Cm7
B♭(add9)/D
G7♯9
neigh - bors might think. Say!
got to get home. (Spoken:) Say, darling,
Ba - by it's bad out there!
Ba - by, you'd freeze out there.

Cm7
F9
Cm7
F7♯9
What's in this drink?
can you lend me your comb?
I
You've
No cabs to be had out there.
It's up to your knees out there.
B♭6
Cm7
B♭(add9)/D
Gm7
G♭9
Fm9
B♭9♯11
wish I knew how to break the spell.
real-ly been grand, but don't you see.
Your eyes are like star-light now
I thrill when you touch my hand.
I'll take your hat.
How can you do
Fm9
B♭13
E9
E♭maj9
D♭9
I ought to say, "No, no, no, sir!"
There's bound to be talk to-mor-row.
At
At
Your hair looks swell.
this thing to me?
Mind if I move in
Think of my life-long

C13
2fr
C7♭13
Cm7/F
8fr
F7
least I'm gon - na say that I tried.
least there will be plen - ty im - plied.
I
I
clos - er?
sor - row
What's the sense of hurt - ing my pride?
if you caught pneu - mo - nia and died.
3
B♭6
A♭13♯11
4fr
G7
real - ly can't stay.
real - ly can't stay.
Ah, but it's
Oh, ba - by, don't hold out.
Get o - ver that old doubt.
Ah, but it's
1
C7
F7♭9
B♭(add9)
6fr
G7♯5(♭9)
C7♯9(♭13)
2fr
F7♯9
7fr
cold out - side.
cold out - side.
3
3

2
B♭6/9
G7♯9
C7♯9
F13
C7
4fr
I
cold
cold
3
E♭m7
6fr
out
out
B♭9
D7♯9
E♭maj9
E7♯5(♭9)
Cm7/F
F7
B♭13♯11
8fr
side.
side.
rit.

Breath of Heaven
(Mary's Song)

Words and Music by
Amy Grant and Chris Eaton

Rubato

Bm Em/G Em Bm Em/G Em

R.H. *L.H.* *p* *8va*

With pedal

Bm Em/G Em Bm Em/G Em

I have

8va

Slowly

Bm Em/B Bm G Em(add2)

trav - eled __ man - y moon - less __ nights, _ cold and
wait - ing __ in a si - lent __ pray'r. _ I am
won - der __ as You watch my __ face, __ if a

Bm Em/B Bm A D

wea - ry ___ with a babe in - side. __ And I
fright - ened __ by the load I ________ bear. __ In a
wis - er ____ one should have had my ________ place? _ But I

Em
Bm
G
Em
Bm
To Coda
wonder what I've done.
world as cold as stone,
of - fer all I am
Ho - ly Fa - ther, You have
must I walk this path a -
for the mer - cy of Your
1
G
Asus2
Gsus2
Asus2
3
come and cho - sen me now to car - ry Your
Bm
Em/G
Em
Bm
Em/G
Em
Son.
I am
R.H.
L.H.
8va
2
G
Asus2
Gsus2
Asus2
lone? Be with me now, be with me

Gsus2
D
Em/D
D
Em/D
F#7/C#
now. Breath of heav - en, hold me to - geth - er. Be for - ev - er
Bm
A/G
D(add2)
D
Em/D
near me, breath of heav - en. Breath of heav - en, light - en my
D
Em/D
F#7/C#
Bm
A/G
Em11
5fr
dark - ness. Pour o - ver me Your ho - li - ness, for You are Ho - ly,
A7sus
Bm
G/B
Bm
Em/G
Em
D.S. al Coda
breath of heav - en.
Do You
8va

CODA
G
Asus2
Gsus2
Asus2
plan. Help me be strong, help me be...
G/B
A/C♯
Dsus2
D
Em/D
help me. Breath of heav - en, hold me to -
D
Em/D
F♯7/C♯
Bm
A/G
D(add2)
geth - er. Be for - ev - er near me, breath of heav - en.
D
Em/D
D
Em/D
F♯7/C♯
Breath of heav - en, light - en my dark - ness. Pour o - ver me Your

1
Bm
A/G
Em11
5fr
A7
ho - li - ness, for You are Ho - ly.
2
Bm
A/G
Em11
5fr
Asus
Dsus2
ho - li - ness, for You are ho - ly, breath of heav - en,
Gsus2/B
Dsus2
Gsus2/B
Dsus2
breath of heav - en, breath of heav - en.
Gsus2/B
D
rit.

Blue Christmas

Words and Music by
Billy Hayes and Jay Johnson

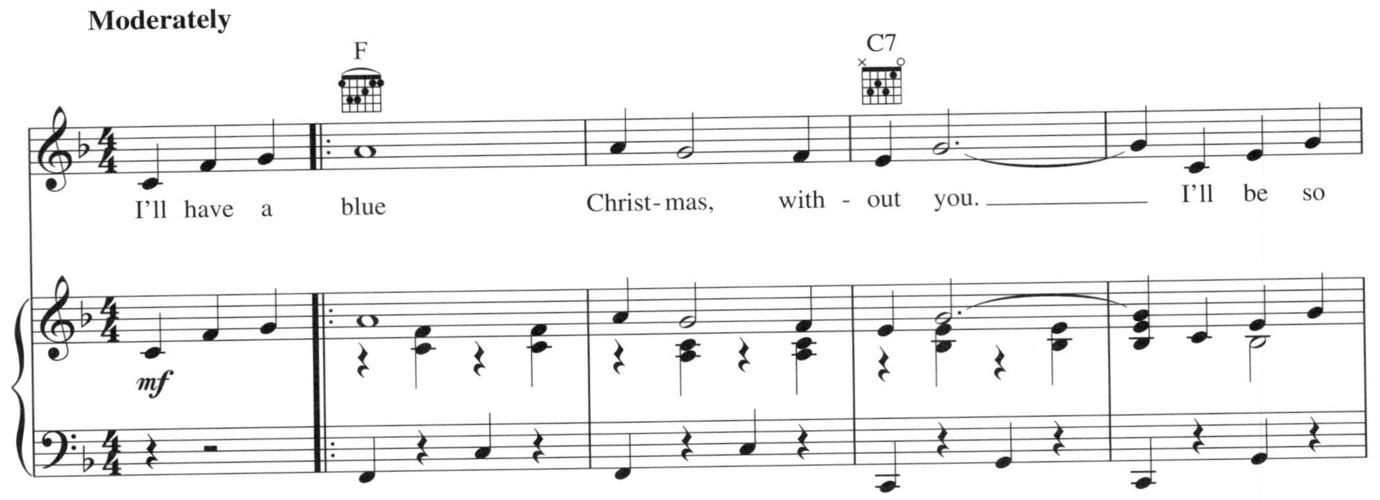

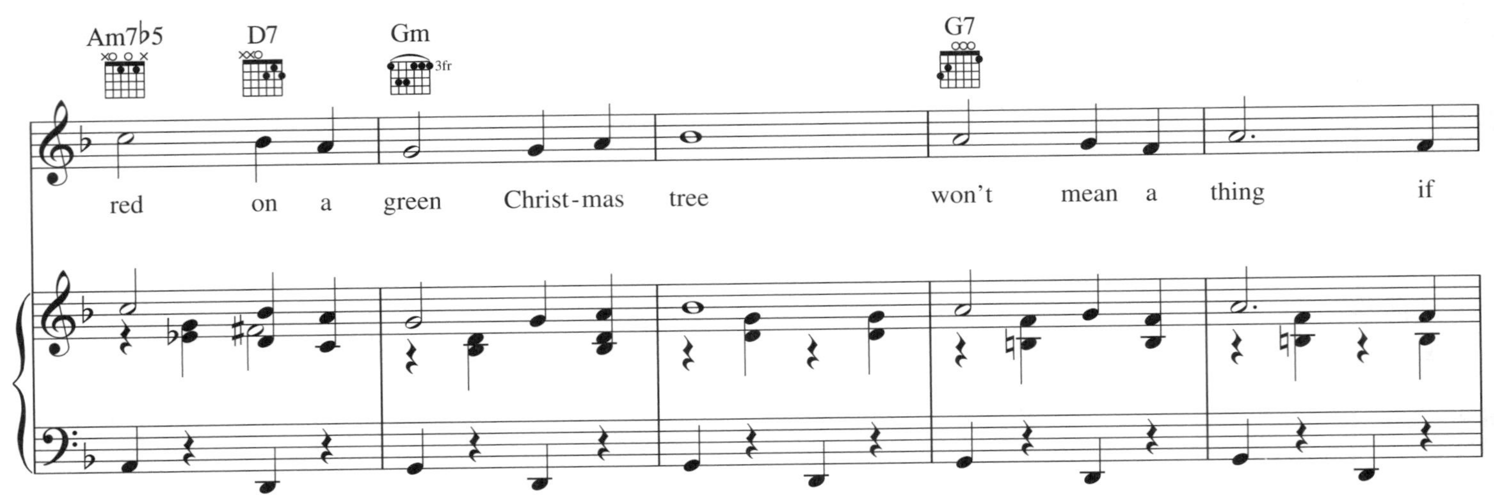

C7
F
C7
you're not here with me. I'll have a blue Christ-mas, that's cer - tain.
And when that blue heart-ache starts hurt - in', you'll be
F
Am7♭5
D7
Am7♭5
D7
Gm
3fr
Bdim7
C7
do - in' all right, with your Christ - mas of white, but I'll have a
blue, blue Christ - mas. I'll have a Christ - mas.
1
F
2
F

Children of Christmas

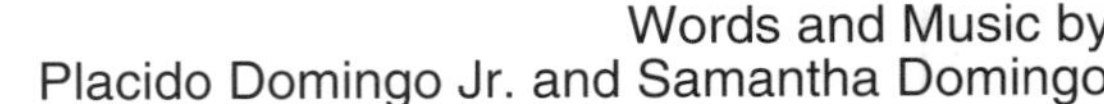
Words and Music by
Placido Domingo Jr. and Samantha Domingo

Moderately slow

B♭ E♭6/G F/E♭ Dm7

mp

E♭ Cm7 E♭/F

cresc.

F7 B♭add2

mf

On a

B♭ C/B♭ E♭/F E♭/A♭

cold mid - win - ter's night, through the dark - ness shines a
can - dles on a tree shine for hope and lib - er -

B♭
C/B♭
light. On a frost - y Christ - mas night, there's a
ty. Christ - mas choirs a - cross the land sing to -
E♭/F
E♭/A♭
B♭
F/A
Gm
love that's burn - ing bright. In each cor - ner of the
geth - er hand in hand. For each child from east to
Dm7
E♭
F
B♭
F/A
world, chil - dren's voic - es can be heard, ask - ing
west, lay our bur - dens down to rest. If our
Gm
Dm7
Csus4
C
God to make things right in a prayer for peace to -
hearts should go a - stray, Christ - mas stars will light the

*From this point, recorded a whole step higher than written.

Cm
3fr
E♭m6
pain, a child of hope is born a - gain. And if the
B♭/F
C/F
E♭/F
world is up - side down, then we can turn it back a -
1.
B♭
E♭/F
round.
Light - ed
2.
B♭
C
Dm
round.
For the chil - dren of

Am
Gm7
3fr
C7
F
C/E
Christ - mas, we should make the fight - ing cease.
Dm
Am
G7sus4
G7
For the chil - dren of Christ - mas, let us turn war in - to peace.
C7
B♭/D
E♭
Dm
3
We can make a new start
C
B♭
F/A
A♭
4fr
with love in our hearts,
for the chil - dren of

B♭
Gm
3fr
A♭
4fr
F9sus4
Christ - mas,
for the chil - dren of
peace.
f
*From this point, recorded a minor 3rd higher than written.
F13
B♭
For ev - 'ry
tear there is a
smile,
if we can
E♭/B♭
F9
Dm7
love for just a
while,
if we can
take a - way the
D♭maj7
4fr
Cm7
3fr
E♭/F
B♭/D
B♭
rage,
if we can
turn an - oth - er
page.
For ev - 'ry

Gm
Cm
Cm/E♭
man who dies in pain, a child of hope is born a -
E♭m6/G♭
B♭/F
C/F
gain. And if the world is up - side down, then we can
F7
A♭
Fm
B♭/D
E♭m/B♭
turn it back a - round,
cresc.
Gm7
B♭/F
B♭
turn it back a - round
ff

Christmas
(Baby Please Come Home)

Words and Music by
Phil Spector, Ellie Greenwich
and Jeff Barry

Gm
3fr
Ab
4fr
(Christ - mas) I'm watch-ing it fall. (Christ - mas) lots of
(Christ - mas) all ring-ing in song. (Christ - mas) full of
Bb7
1
peo - ple a - round. (Christ - mas) Ba - by please come home.
hap - py sounds. (Christ - mas) Ba - by please
2
Eb
3fr
come home. They're sing - ing "Deck The Halls,"
Cm
3fr
Ab
4fr
but it's not like Christ-mas at all. 'Cause I re - mem - ber when

B♭7
you were here
and all the fun we had last year.
E♭
3fr
Gm
3fr
(Christ - mas) Pret - ty lights on the tree, (Christ - mas) I'm
Instrumental solo
(Christ - mas) If there was a way (Christ - mas) I'd
A♭
4fr
To Coda
watch - ing them shine. (Christ - mas) You should be here with me.
hold back this tear. (Christ - mas) But it's Christ - mas day.
B♭7
1
2
D.S. al Coda
(Christ - mas) Ba - by please come home.
Solo ends

CODA
B♭7
(Please) Please, (Please) please, (Please) please, (Please) please,
(Please) Ba - by please come home.
E♭
(Christ - mas)
Lead vocal ad lib.
Cm
(Christ - mas)
A♭
(Christ - mas)
B♭7
(Christ - mas)
Repeat and Fade

Christmas Is All Around

Words and Music by
Reg Presley

F
Gm
3fr
B♭
C
writ - ten in the wind, it's ev - 'ry - where I go.
gave your pres - ents to me, and I gave mine to you.
So if you real - ly love Christ - mas,
I need San - ta be - side me,
come on and let it snow.
in ev - 'ry - thing I do.
1st time only
2nd time only
Dm
C7
F/C

B♭
Gm
3fr
(1.,2.) You know I love Christ - mas, I al - ways will;
(D.S.) Instrumental
E♭
3fr
C
my mind's made up, the way that I feel.
B♭
Gm
3fr
G7
There's no be - gin - ning, there'll be no end, 'cause on Christ - mas you
C
C/B♭
To Coda
1
C/A
C/G
2
C/A
C/G
D.S. al Coda
can de - pend. You

CODA
C/A
C/G
F5
F5/G
It's writ - ten in the wind,
Bbsus2
C7sus
F
Gm
3fr
Bb
C
it's ev-'ry-where I go. _
So
F
Gm
3fr
Bb
C
Dm
F/C
if you real - ly love _ me,
come on and let it show. _
Bb
C
Dm
F/C
Bb
C
Come on and let it show. _
So

Dm
F/C
B♭
C
if you real - ly love me,
come on and let it...
Dm
F/C
B♭
C
If you real - ly love me,
come on and let it... Now
Dm
F/C
C
if you real - ly love me,
come on and let it show.
F
Gm
3fr
C5
3fr
B♭
F

The Christmas Song
(Chestnuts Roasting on an Open Fire)

Music and Lyric by
Mel Torme and Robert Wells

Eb6 Bb7 Eb6 Bb9 Eb6 Eb9
knows a tur - key and some mis - tle - toe help to make the sea - son
Ab Ab7 G7#5 Cm Cm/Bb Abm6 Eb/Bb Am7 D7
4fr 4fr 3fr 8fr 4fr 6fr
3
bright. Ti - ny tots with their eyes all a - glow will
Gm7 C7 Fm7 Bb7 Eb6 Bbm7 Eb9
find it hard to sleep to - night. They know that San - ta's on his
Bbm7 Eb9 Bbm7 Eb9 Abmaj7
way; he's load - ed lots of toys and good - ies on his sleigh, and ev - 'ry

A♭m7 D♭9 G♭maj7 Cm7 F7
4fr 3fr
3 3
moth-er's child is gon - na spy to see if rein - deer real - ly know how to
B♭7sus B♭7 E♭6 B♭7 E♭6 B♭9
fly. And so I'm of - fer - ing this sim - ple phrase to
E♭6 E♭9 A♭ A♭7 G7♯5 Cm Cm/B♭ A♭m6
4fr 4fr 3fr 8fr 4fr
kids from one to nine - ty - two. Al - though it's been said man - y
E♭/B♭ Am7 A♭9 E♭/B♭ Cm7 Fm7 B♭7♭9
6fr 4fr 6fr 3fr
1 E♭6 Fm7/B♭ B♭13♭9
6fr
2 E♭6/9
5fr
times, man - y ways, "Mer - ry Christ - mas to you." you."
rit.
a tempo

Christmas Stays the Same

Words and Music by
Jack Murphy and Frank Wildhorn

Fmaj9
Fm9
Bm7♭5
E7♭9
Ev - 'ry - one is hap - py that it's here. For we
wish - ing you were just a kid a - gain. For we
Am
C7/G
F
Fm6
all re - mem - ber some past De - cem - ber of
all re - mem - ber some past De - cem - ber of
Em7
Am9
Dm7add4
1.
G7♯5
tin - sel and hol - ly and peo - ple we love.
train sets that whis - tled and dolls we could
2.
G7♯5
Fmaj7
D7♭9
Dm11
B♭9♯11
C9
name. Oh, the years may change, but Christ - mas stays the same.
rit.

Slower
Bb/C
C6
Bb/C
C
Bb/C
C6
Fmaj7
Tur - key and gra - vy and hams full of hon - ey, cous - ins you see once a year,
Ab/Bb
Bb6
Ab/Bb
Bb
Ab/Bb
Bb
fa - thers who scold you then slip you some mon - ey, and roofs full of ti - ny rein -
Tempo I
Bm7b5
E7
Am
C7/G
deer. Yes, we all re - mem - ber some
F
Fm6
Em7
past De - cem - ber of grand - ma's and

Freely, slowly

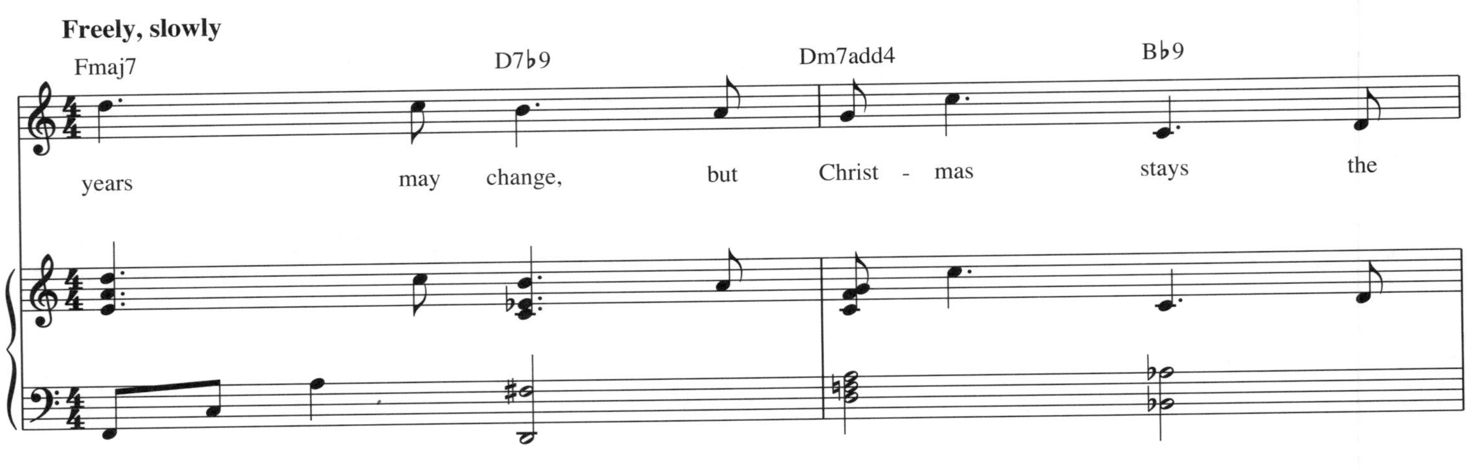

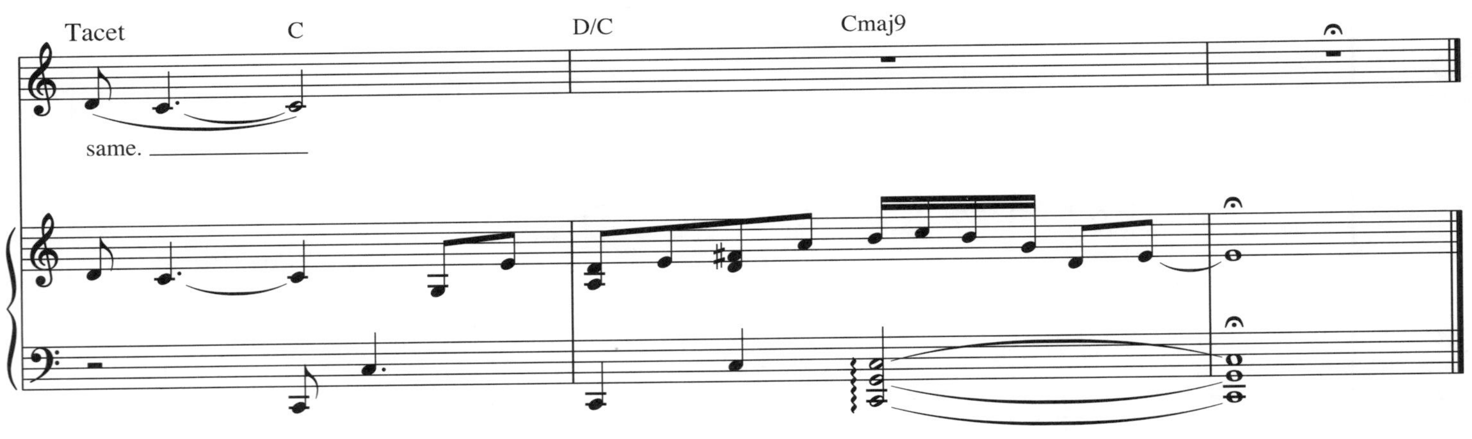

Christmas Time Is Here

from A CHARLIE BROWN CHRISTMAS

Words by Lee Mendelson

Music by Vince Guaraldi

D♭maj7
G♭13♯11
D♭maj7
G♭13♯11
Sleigh-bells in the air, beau-ty ev - 'ry - where.
3
3
Am7
E♭9
D9
4fr
D7♭9
4fr
Gm7
D♭9
C13
2fr
C13♭9
3fr
yule-tide by the fire - side and joy-ful mem - 'ries there.
Fmaj9
E♭13♯11
6fr
Fmaj9
E♭13♯11
6fr
Christ-mas time is here, well be draw - ing near.
3
3
3
3
3
To Coda
Bm7♭5
B♭m7
Am7
A♭m7
4fr
Gm7
B♭/C
Fmaj9
Oh, that we could al - ways see such spir - it though the year.
3
3

Eb13#11
Fmaj9
Eb13#11
Bm7b5
Bbm7
Am7
Abm7
Gm7
Bb/C
Fmaj9
Eb13#11
Fmaj9
Eb13#11
Bm7b5
Bbm7
Am7
Abm7
Gm7
Bb/C
Fmaj9
D.S. al Coda
CODA
Fmaj9
year.

The Christmas Waltz

Words by Sammy Cahn

Music by Jule Styne

C9
C7♭9
Fmaj7
Dm7
G9
9fr
G7♭5/D♭
8fr
sleigh with things, things for you and for
C7
C7♯5
8fr
F
D7sus
D7
Gm7
me. It's that time of year, when the world falls in
C7
F
D7♭9
4fr
Gm
3fr
love, ev - 'ry song you hear seems to say:
C7♭9
F
Gm7
"Mer - ry Christ - mas, may your New Year

C9
Am7♭5
D7
D7♯5
D7
dreams come true." And this
G9
9fr
C9
C7
F
song of mine, in three - quar - ter time,
D7
G7
Cm7
3fr
C7
wish - es you and yours the same thing
F
Dm
Gm7
C9
F
C5/F
F
too.
poco rall.

Do You Hear What I Hear

Words and Music by
Noel Regney and Gloria Shayne

Am
Em
F
G
F
star, a star, danc - ing in the night, with a tail as big as a
song, a song, high a - bove the tree, with a voice as big as the
Child, a Child shiv - ers in the cold; let us bring Him sil - ver and
E
Am
G
F
C/E
Dm7
G
C
Gm7
kite, with a tail as big as a kite."
sea, with a voice as big as the sea."
gold, let us bring Him sil - ver and gold."
1, 2
C
3
C
Gm7
Said the
Said the
Said the king to the peo - ple ev - 'ry -
C
where, "Lis - ten to what I say!

Gm7
C
Pray for peace, peo - ple ev - 'ry - where, lis - ten to what I say!
Am
Em
The Child, the Child, sleep - ing in the night, He will
F
G
F
E
Am
G
F
C/E
Dm7
G7
opt.
bring us good - ness and light, He will bring us good - ness and
mf
C
Gm7
C
Gm7
C
light."
rall.

Deck the Hall

Traditional Welsh Carol

2. See the blazing yule before us. Fa la la *etc.*
Strike the harp and join the chorus. Fa la la *etc.*
Follow me in merry measure. Fa la la *etc.*
While I tell of yuletide treasure. Fa la la *etc.*

3. Fast away the old year passes. Fa la la *etc.*
Hail the new, ye lads and lasses. Fa la la *etc.*
Sing we joyous all together. Fa la la *etc.*
Heedless of the wind and weather. Fa la la *etc.*

Fairytale of New York

Words and Music by
Jem Finer and Shane MacGowan

1
Gsus
C
G7sus
2
Gsus
C
F/C
G7/C
C
F/C
Gsus
bout you. 2. Got on a dreams come true.
Medium fast
C
G
C
F
G
C
Female: 3. They got
G
Am
F
C
cars big as bars, they got riv - ers of gold; but the wind goes right through you, it's no
G
C
Am
C
F
place for the old. When you first took my hand on a cold Christ - mas Eve, you

C
G
C
prom-ised me Broad-way was wait-ing for me.
Male:
4. You were hand-some, You were pret-ty, Queen
5. (See additional lyrics)
G
C
F
G
C
of New York Cit-y.
Both:
When the band fin-ished play-ing, they howled out for more. Si-
G
C
F
na-tra was swing-ing; all the drunks, they were sing-ing. We kissed on the cor-ner, then
G
C
F
danced through the night. The boys of the N-Y-P-D choir were

C/E
Am
C
F
G
sing-ing "Gal - way Bay." And the bells were ring-ing out for Christ-mas Day.
1
C
G
Am
F
C
G
C
Am
C
F
C
G
C
Female: 5. You're a
2
C
F

C
F
G
C
G
Male: 6. I could have
been some - one.
Female: Well, so could an - y - one.
You took my dreams
from me when I first found you.
Gsus
3fr
Male: I kept them
with me, babe; I put them with my own.
Can't make it

Additional Lyrics

2. Got on a lucky one, came in eighteen to one;
   I've got a feeling this year's for me and you.
   So happy Christmas; I love you, baby.
   I can see a better time, when all our dreams come true.

5. *(Female)* You're a bum, you're a punk!
   (Male) You're an old slut on junk
   Lying there almost dead on a drip in that bed!
   (Female) You scumbag! You maggot!
   You cheap lousy faggot!
   Happy Christmas your arse!
   I pray God it's our last.

Feliz Navidad

Music and Lyrics by
José Feliciano

1
2
3
A7
D
N.C.
a - ño y fe - li - ci - dad.
Fe - liz Na - vi -
To next strain
I want to wish you a
Fine
G
Mer - ry Christ - mas, with lots of pres - ents to
make you hap - py. I want to wish you a Mer - ry Christ - mas from the

A7
Em7
A7
D
G
D
bot - tom of my heart. I want to wish you a
G
A7
D
Mer - ry Christ - mas, with mis - tle - toe and lots of cheer.
G
With lots of laugh - ter through - out the years from the
A7
Em7
A7
D
G
D
N.C.
D.S. al Fine
bot - tom of my heart. Fe - liz Na - vi -

Frosty the Snow Man

Words and Music by
Steve Nelson and Jack Rollins

F F♯dim7 C/G F F♯dim7
fair - y tale, they say; he was made of snow but the
broom - stick in his hand, run - ning here and there all a -
C/G A Dm7 G7 C C7
chil - dren know how he came to life one day. There
round the square say - in', "Catch me if you can." He
F F♯dim7 C/G A7 Dm7 G7 C
must have been some mag - ic in that old silk hat they found, for
led them down the streets of town right to the traf - fic cop, and he
G A♭dim7 Am7 D9 G G7♯5
6fr
4fr
when they placed it on his head he be - gan to dance a - round. Oh,
on - ly paused a mo - ment when he heard him hol - ler, "Stop!" For

C
C7
F
F♯dim7
C/G
Fros - ty the Snow Man was a - live as he could be, and the
Fros - ty the Snow Man had to hur - ry on his way, but he
F
F♯dim7
C/G
A
Dm7
G7
C
chil - dren say he could laugh and play just the same as you and me.
waved good - bye say - in', "Don't you cry, I'll be back a - gain some - day."
G7
Thump - et - y thump thump, thump - et - y thump thump, look at Fros - ty go.
lightly
C
Thump - et - y thump thump, thump - et - y thump thump, o - ver the hills of snow.

The Gift

Words and Music by
Tom Douglas and Jim Brickman

B♭
F/A
Gm
3fr
B♭/F
Sit - ting by the fire we made, you're the an - swer when I prayed
E♭
3fr
B♭/D
Cm7
3fr
F7sus
I would find some - one and ba - by, I found you.
F
B♭/D
E♭
3fr
Fsus
All I want is to hold you for - ev - er.
F
B♭/D
E♭
3fr
Fsus
All I need is you more ev - 'ry day.

F
B♭/D
D7
You saved my heart from be - ing
Gm
Gm/F
Em7♭5
Cm7
3fr
B♭/D
bro - ken a - part. You gave your love a - way and I'm thank - ful
F7sus
B♭
F(add4)/A
ev - 'ry day for the gift.
Gm
F6
E♭(add9)
6fr

F
C/E
Dm
F/C
Male: Watch-ing as you soft - ly sleep, what I'd give if I could keep
B♭(add9)
6fr
F/A
Gm
3fr
C
just this mo - ment, if on - ly time stood still.
3
F
C/E
Dm
F/C
But the col-ors fade a - way and the years will make us grey,
B♭
F/A
Gm
3fr
C7sus
but, ba - by, in my eyes, you'll still be beau - ti - ful.

C
F/A
B♭
Csus
3fr
Both: All I want is to hold you for - ev - er.
C
F/A
B♭
Csus
3fr
All I need is you more ev - 'ry day.
To Coda
C
F/A
A7
Dm
Dm/C
Male: You saved my heart from be - ing bro - ken a - part.
a - part.
Bm7♭5
Gm7
F/A
C7sus
Female: You gave your love a - way
Male: and I'm thank - ful ev - 'ry day

F
B♭
Both: for the gift.
C
Dm
F/A
B♭(add9)
6fr
F/A
Gm7
C
Csus
3fr
B♭/D
C/E
F
B♭
Gm7
F/A
Csus
3fr
C
D.S. al Coda
Both: All I want

CODA
Bm7♭5
Gm7
Female: You gave your love a - way.
F/A
B♭
C/D
Dm
Gm7
Male: I can't find the words to say Female: that I'm thank - ful ev - 'ry day
rit.
Csus
F
C(add9)/E
Dm
Both: for the gift.
a tempo
C6
B♭(add9)
Csus
F(add9)
Female: Ooh, ah. Male: Ah, ooh, ooh.
rit.

The Greatest Gift of All

Words and Music by
John Jarvis

Moderately slow

D D7/C G/B C G/D D7 G C/G

mf

D/G C/G G D/F♯ G

Dawn is slow - ly break - ing,

C G D/F♯

our friends have all gone home. You and I are

Em A7 D

wait - ing for San - ta Claus to come.

G
D/F#
G
G7
C
D/C
C
There's a pres - ent by the tree,
stock-ings on the
wall.
D
D/C
G/B
Know-ing you're in love with me is the
G/D
D7
C/G
G/A
3fr
G7/B
great - est gift of all.
C7
F
The fire is slow - ly fad - ing,
chill is in the

C
G/B
Am
air.
All the gifts are wait - ing
D7
G
F/A
G/B
C
G/B
for chil-dren ev - 'ry - where.
Through the win - dow
C
C7
F
C
I can see
snow be - gin to fall.
G
G/F
C/E
F
C/G
G
Know-ing you're in love with me
is the great - est gift of

C
A7
G/B
A7/C♯
D
A/C♯
all.
Just be - fore I
D
G
D
go to sleep
I hear a church bell ring.
A/C♯
Bm
Bm7
E7
Mer - ry Christ - mas ev - 'ry - one
is the song it
A
G/B
A7/C♯
D
A/C♯
D
sings.
So I say a si - lent prayer

G
D
A7
A7/G
for crea-tures great and small.
Peace on earth good _
D7/F#
G
D/A
A7
D
will to men is the great - est gift of _ all.
A7
A7/G
D7/F#
G
D/A
A
Peace on earth good _ will to men is the great - est gift
D
G
A9
5fr
D
of _ all. _
rit.

Go, Tell It on the Mountain

African-American Spiritual
Verses by John W. Work, Jr.

D C C7 G
asked the Lord to help me And He showed me the way:
asked the Lord to help me And He taught me how to pray.
God sent out sal - va - tion That bless - ed Christ - mas morn.
G C G D7 C
Go tell it on the moun - tain, O - ver the hills and
G C G C G
ev - 'ry - where, Go tell it on the moun - tain, Our
1. 2.
G D7 G C G
Je - sus Christ is born.
3.
G D7 G C G
Je - sus Christ is born.
much slower

God Rest Ye Merry, Gentlemen

19th Century English Carol

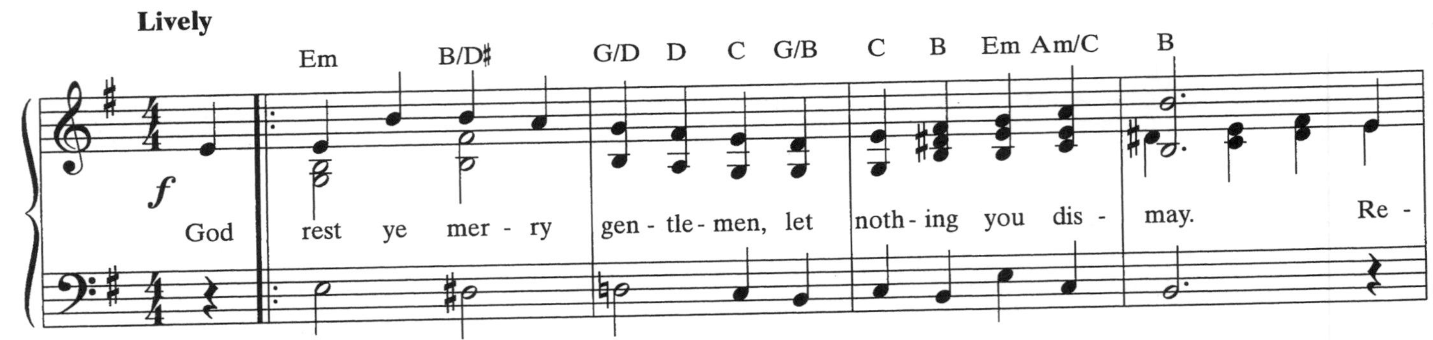

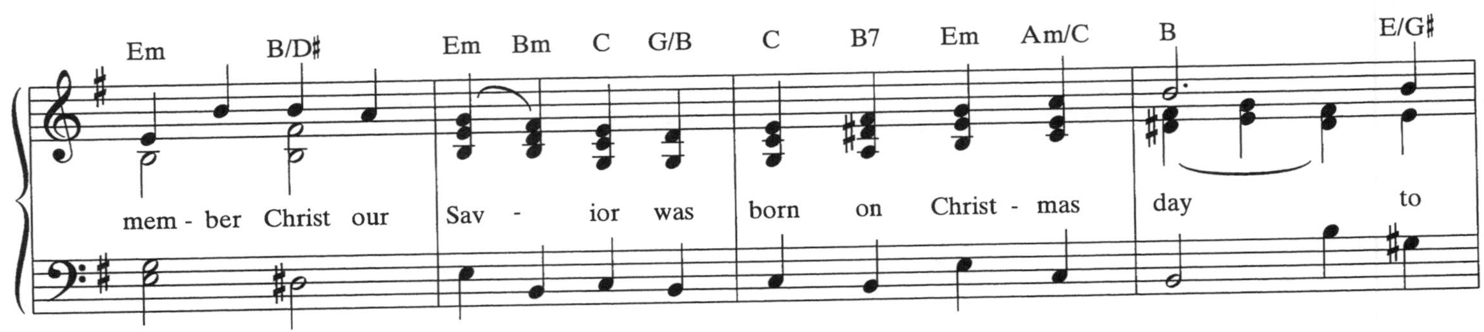

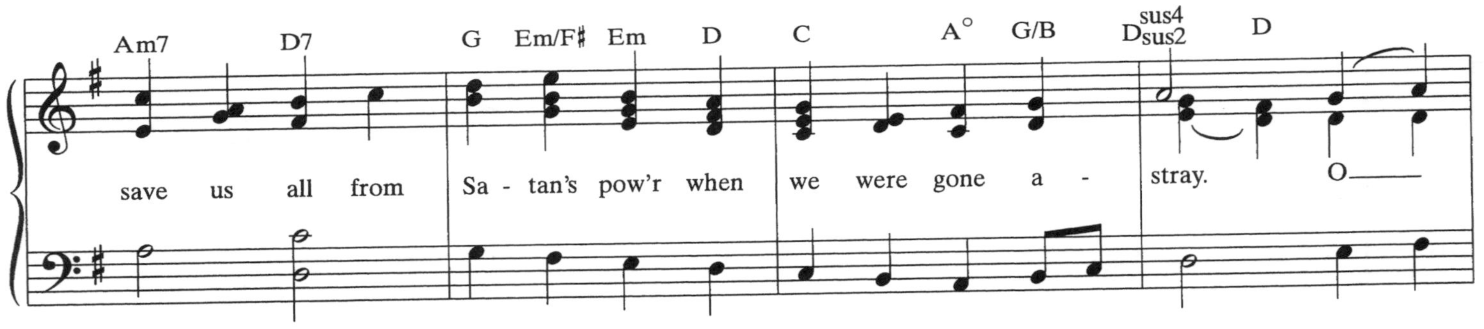

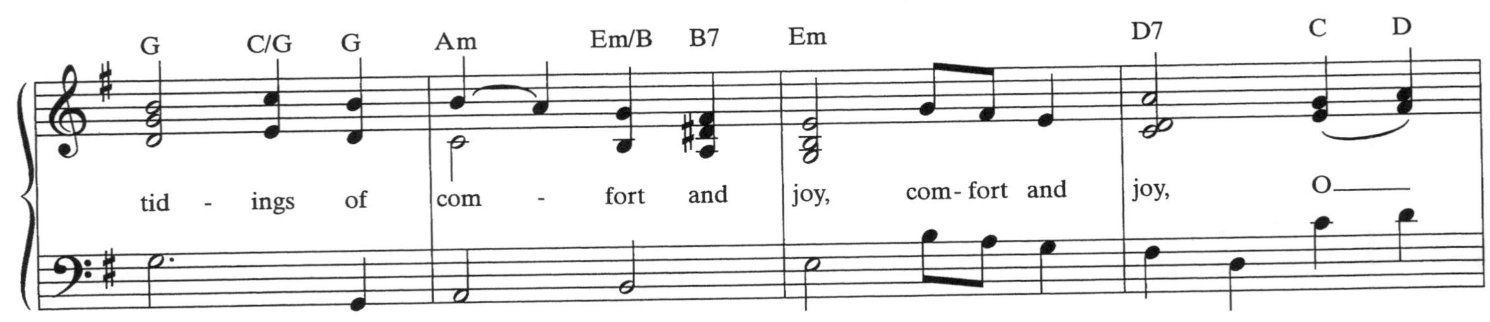

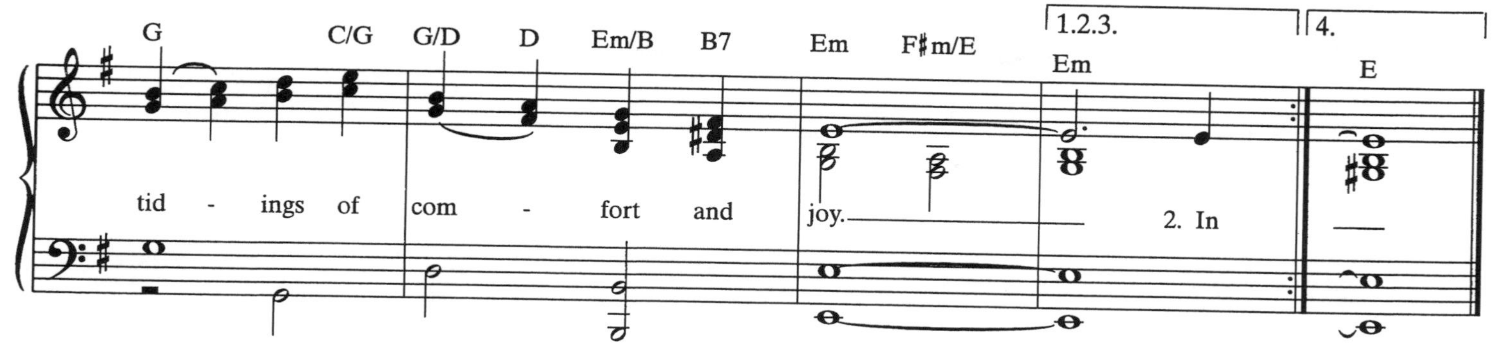

2. In Bethlehem, in Jewry, this blessed Babe was born,
   And laid within a manger, upon this blessed morn.
   The which His mother Mary did nothing take in scorn.
   O, tidings *etc.*

3. From God our Heavenly Father, a blessed Angel came,
   And unto certain shepherds brought tidings of the same.
   How that in Bethlehem was born the Son of God by name.
   O, tidings *etc.*

4. The shepherds at those tidings rejoiced much in mind,
   And left their flocks a-feeding in tempest, storm, and wind,
   And went to Bethlehem straightway, the Son of God to find.
   O, tidings *etc.*

Grandma Got Run Over by a Reindeer

Words and Music by
Randy Brooks

E
D
A
E
B
lieve.
1. She'd been drink - ing too much egg - nog
2.,3. (See additional lyrics)
E
E7
and we begged her not to go,
but she for - got her med - i -
A
B
E
ca - tion,
and she stag - gered out the door in - to the snow.
C♯m
G♯m
B7
4fr
When we found her Christ - mas morn - ing
at the scene of the at -

E
E7
A
tack, she had hoof-prints on her fore-head, and in-
B
1, 2
E
3
E
D.S. al Coda
crim-i-nat-ing Claus marks on her back.
elves.
CODA
E
C♯
F♯
lieve.
Grand-ma got run o-ver by a
B
rein-deer walk-ing home from our house Christ-mas Eve.

Additional Lyrics

2. Now we're all so proud of Grandpa,
He's been taking this so well.
See him in there watching football,
Drinking beer and playing cards with Cousin Mel.
It's not Christmas without Grandma.
All the family's dressed in black,
And we just can't help but wonder:
Should we open up her gifts or send them back?
Chorus

3. Now the goose is on the table,
And the pudding made of fig,
And the blue and silver candles,
That would just have matched the hair in Grandma's wig.
I've warned all my friends and neighbors,
Better watch out for yourselves.
They should never give a license
To a man who drives a sleigh and plays with elves.
Chorus

Happy Holiday

from the Motion Picture Irving Berlin's HOLIDAY INN

Words and Music by
Irving Berlin

Fm7
hol - i - day, happy holiday.
8va
Bb7
Eb
Cm7
May the cal - en - dar keep bring - ing hap - py
Fm7
Bb7
Eb
F7
Bb6
hol - i - days to you. Hap - py hol - i - day,
Cm7
F7
hap - py hol - i - day. While the

Cm7
F7
B♭6
Gm7
Cm7
F7
mer - ry bells keep ring - ing, may your ev - 'ry wish come
B♭6
true. Hap - py hol - i - day, hap - py
8va
Cm7
F7
Cm7
F7
hol - i - day. May the cal - en - dar keep
8va
B♭6
Gm7
Cm7
F7
B♭6
bring - ing hap - py hol - i - days to you.

Happy Xmas
(War Is Over)

Words and Music by
John Lennon and Yoko Ono

Em
A
fun, the near and the dear ones, the old and the
fun, the near and the dear ones, the old and the
D
G
young. A mer - ry, mer-ry X - mas and a hap - py New
young.
A
Em
G
To Coda
year. Let's hope it's a good one with - out an - y
D
E
A
fear. And so this is X - mas for weak and for
(War is o - ver

Bm
E
strong. The rich and the poor ones, the road is so
if you want it; war is o - ver
A
D
long. And so, hap - py X - mas for black and for
now.
War is o - ver
Em
A
white, for the yel - low and red ones; let's stop all the
if you want it; war is o - ver
D
G
fights. A mer - ry, mer - ry X - mas and a hap - py New
now.)

A
Em
G
Year. Let's hope it's a good one ___ with - out an - y
D
E
D.S. al Coda
fear. And so this is
Coda
D
E
fear
A
Bm
War is o - ver if you want it;
E
A
war is o - ver now. ___

Have Yourself a Merry Little Christmas

Words and Music by
Hugh Martin and Ralph Blane

Am7
Em/G
Am6
B7
Em
G/D
Am7/D
D9
4fr
But the wel - kin will ring one day, and that day will be
G7sus
G7
C
Am7
Dm7
F/G
G7
soon. Have your - self a mer - ry lit - tle Christ - mas,
rit.
a tempo
C
Am
G7sus
G7
C
Am7
let your heart be light. From now on our
Dm7
G7
E7
A7
D9
4fr
G7
trou - bles will be out of sight.

C
Am
Dm7
F/G
G7
C
Am
Have your - self a mer - ry lit - tle Christ - mas, make the Yule - tide
G7sus
G7
C
Am7
Dm7
E7
gay. From now on our trou - bles will be miles a -
Am7
C7
C7♭9
C7♯5
8fr
Fmaj9
Fm
way.
Here we are as in
cresc.
mf
C/E
E♭dim7
Dm7
F/G
G+
3fr
C
Am7
old - en days, hap - py gold - en days of yore.

F#m7b5
B13
B7#5
Em
A7
G/D
D7sus
D7
Faith - ful friends who are dear to us gath - er near to us once
G7sus
G7
C
Am
Dm7
F/G
G7
more. Through the years we all will be to - geth - er,
dim.
mp
C
G7sus
G7
C
Am7
if the fates al - low. Hang a shin - ing
Dm7
E7b9
E7
Am
C7
C7b9
C7#5
star up - on the high - est bough, and
cresc.

Fmaj9
Am/E
Dm7
Dm7/G
G7♭9
C
Am
A♭m7
4fr
have your - self a mer - ry lit - tle Christ - mas now.
mf
Gm7
C7♭9
Fmaj9
Fm
C/E
E♭dim7
Here we are as in old - en days, hap - py
Dm7
G7sus
G7♯5
Cmaj7
Am9
5fr
F♯m7♭5
4fr
B13
7fr
B7♯5
gold - en days of yore. Faith - ful friends who are
Em
C♯m7♭5
4fr
G/D
D7sus
D7
G7sus
G7
dear to us gath - er near to us once more.
rit. e dim.

C
Am
Dm7
F/G
G7
C
Am
Through the years we all will be to - geth - er, if the fates al -
mp a tempo
G7sus
G7
C
Am7
Dm7
E7♭9
low. Hang a shin - ing star up - on the high - est
Am(add9)
5fr
Am
C13
2fr
C7♭9
C7♯5
8fr
Fmaj9
Am7
bough, and have your - self a
cresc.
f
Dm7
Dm7/G
G7♭9
C
Dm7/G
Cmaj7
mer - ry lit - tle Christ - mas now.
dim.
p

A Holly Jolly Christmas

Music and Lyrics by
Johnny Marks

C♯dim7
G7
Christ - mas, and when you walk down the street,
C♯dim7
G7
say hel - lo to friends you know and ev - 'ry - one you
C
F
Em
F
meet. Oh, ho, the mis - tle - toe hung where you can
C
Dm
Am
D7
C/D
D7
see. Some - bod - y waits for you, kiss her once for

G7
C
me. Have a hol - ly jol - ly Christ - mas, and in
C♯dim7
G7
case you did - n't hear,
oh, by gol - ly, have a
C
1
D7
G7
C
G7
hol - ly jol - ly Christ - mas this year. Have a
2
D7
G7
C
Dm7
G7
C
Christ - mas this year.

Hark! The Herald Angels Sing

Words by Charles Wesley

Music by Felix Mendelssohn-Bartholdy

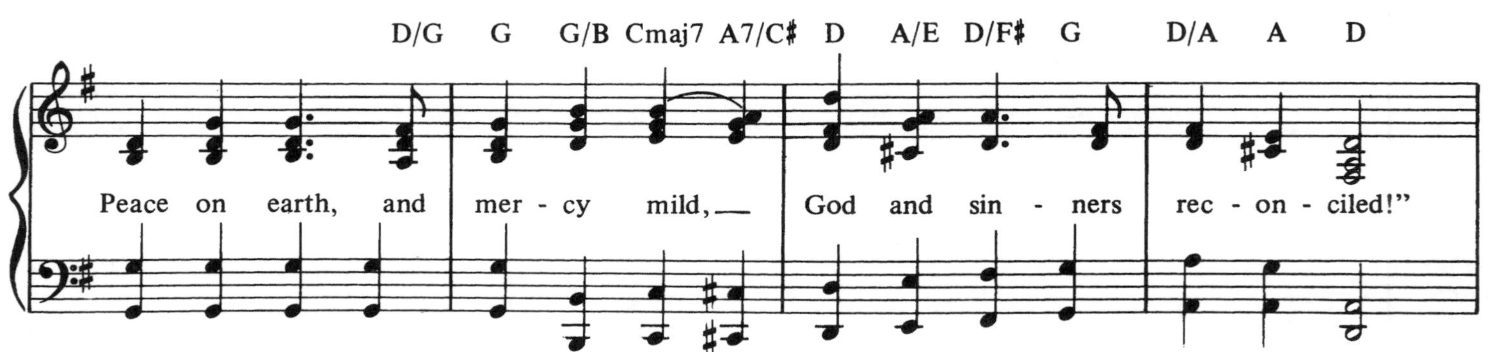

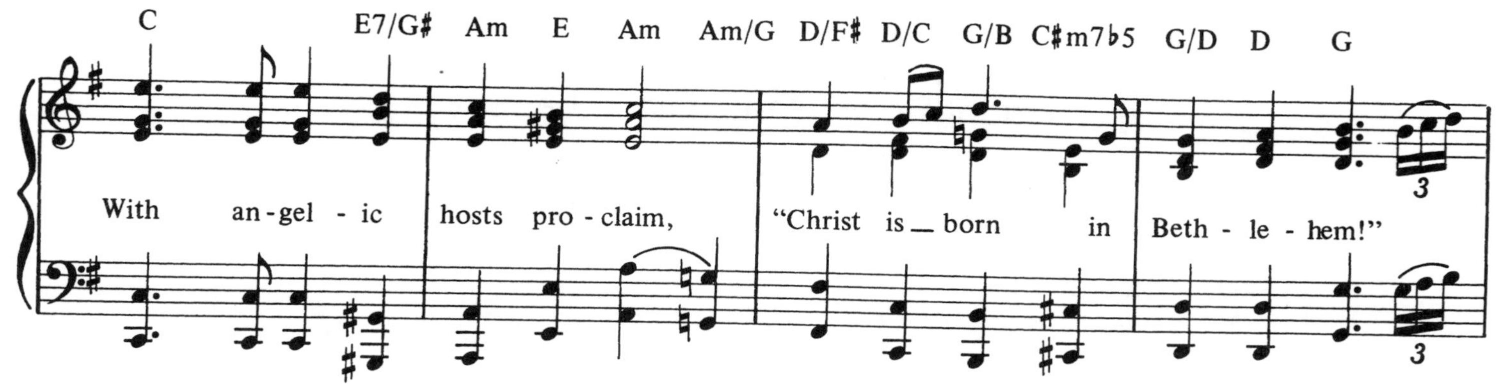

2. Christ, by highest Heaven above, Christ, the everlasting Lord.
Late in time behold Him come, offspring of the favored one.
Veiled in flesh, the Godhead see; hail th'incarnate Deity.
Pleased, as man with men to dwell, Jesus, our Immanuel!
Hark! the herald angels sing, "Glory to the newborn King!"

3. Hail! the Heaven-born Prince of Peace! Hail! the Son of Righteousness!
Light and life to all He brings, ris'n with healing in His wings.
Mild He lays His glory by, born that man no more may die.
Born to raise the sons of earth, born to give them second birth.
Hark! the herald angels sing, "Glory to the newborn King!"

Here Comes Santa Claus
(Right Down Santa Claus Lane)

Words and Music by
Gene Autry and Oakley Haldeman

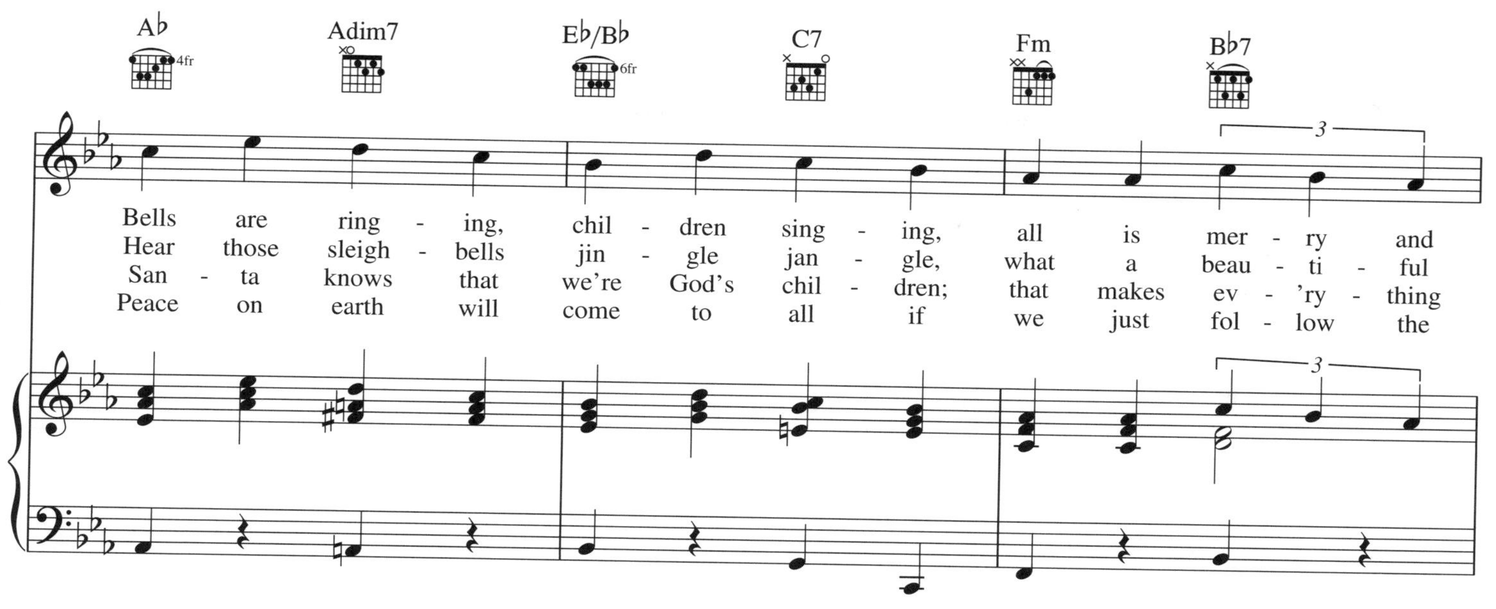
Ab
Adim7
Eb/Bb
C7
Fm
Bb7
Bells are ring - ing, chil - dren sing - ing, all is mer - ry and
Hear those sleigh - bells jin - gle jan - gle, what a beau - ti - ful
San - ta knows that we're God's chil - dren; that makes ev - 'ry - thing
Peace on earth will come to all if we just fol - low the

Eb
Ab
Adim7
Eb/Bb
C7
bright. Hang your stock - ings and say your pray'rs,
sight. Jump in bed, cov - er up your head,
right. Fill your hearts with a Christ - mas cheer,
light. Let's give thanks to the Lord a - bove,
'cause

1-3
Fm
Bb7
Eb
Bb7sus
4
Fm
Bb7
Eb
San - ta Claus comes to - night.
San - ta Claus comes to - night.

The Holiday Season

Words and Music by
Kay Thompson

To Coda
D7 F/G C6 D7 F/G C6
com - in' down the chim - ney, down. (He'll be com - in' down the chim - ney, down.)
com - in' down the chim - ney, down. (When he's com - in' down the chim - ney, down.)
com - in' down the chim - ney, down. (He'll be com - in' down the chim - ney, down.)
1 2
F/C C
It's the He'll have a big fat pack up -
F/C C F/C C F/C C
on his back and lots of good - ies for you and for me. So leave a
F/C C F/C C D7
pep - per - mint stick for old Saint Nick hang - in' on the Christ - mas tree.

G9
9fr
D.S. al Coda
It's the
CODA
He'll have a big fat pack up - on
F
C/E
Dm7
C
his back and lots of good - ies for you and for me. So leave a
pep - per - mint stick for old Saint Nick hang - in' on the Christ - mas tree.
D7
It's the hol - i - day sea - son. So,
C6

Dm7
G13
3fr
Dm7
G13
3fr
Dm7
G13
3fr
whoop - de - doo and dick - o - ry dock, a - don't for - get to
Em7
A7
Dm7
G13
3fr
C6
A7
hang up your sock, 'cause just ex - act - ly at twelve o' clock he'll be
D7
F/G
D7
F/G
D7
com - in' down the chim - ney, com - in' down the chim - ney, com -
F/G
C6
- in' down the chim - ney, down.

(There's No Place Like)

Home For the Holidays

Words and Music by
Al Stillman and Robert Allen

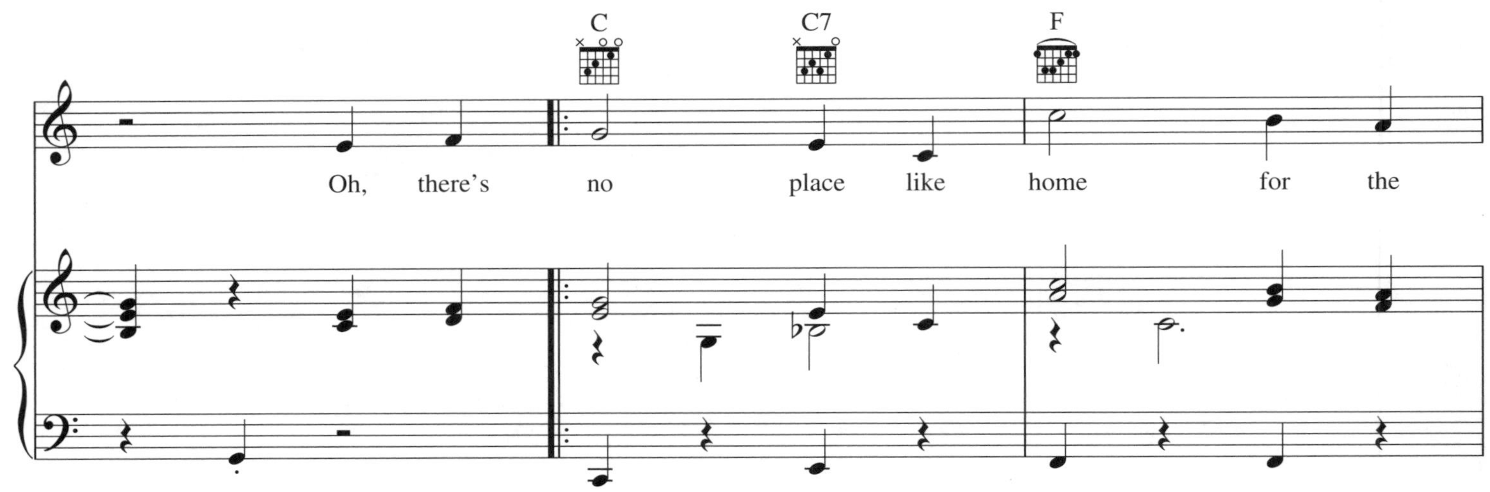

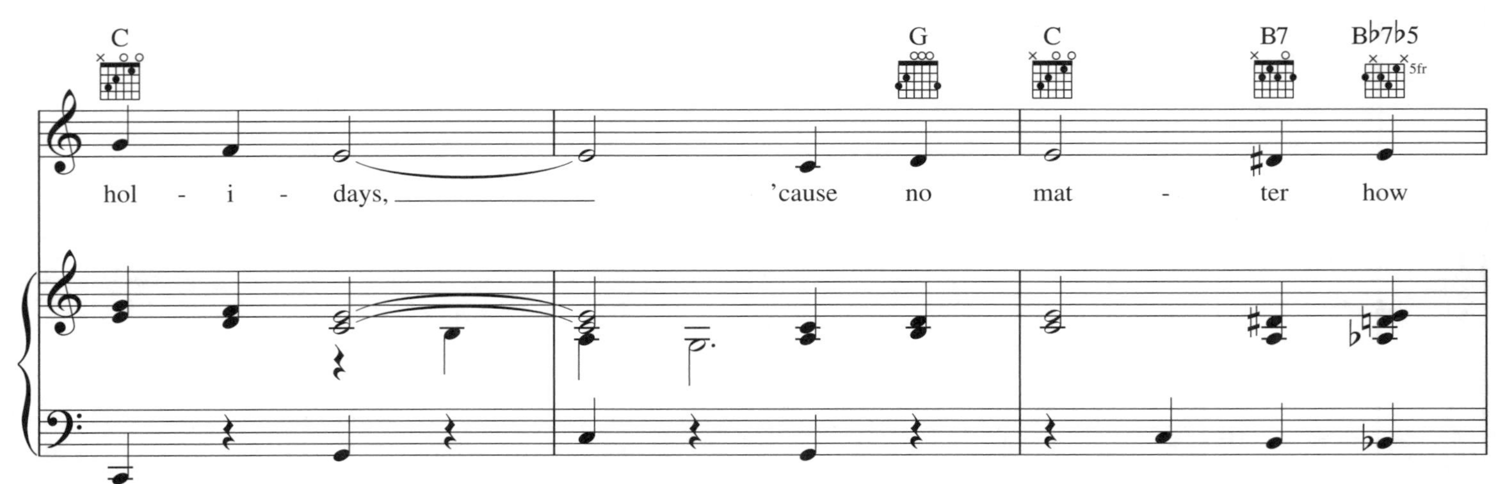

A7
D7
D7♭5
G7
far a - way you roam,
when you
C
C7
F
F♯dim7
C/G
pine for the sun - shine of a friend - ly gaze,
F♯dim7
G7
Dm7
G7
for the hol - i - days you can't beat home, sweet
C
B♭/C
C7
F
home.
I met a man who lives in
A home that knows your joy and

F♯dim7 C/G C♯dim7
Ten - nes - see and he was head - in' for Penn - syl -
laugh - ter filled with mem - 'ries by the score is a
G7 C
van - ia and some home - made pump - kin pie.
home you're glad to wel - come with your heart.
C7 B♭/C C7 F
From Penn - syl - van - ia folks are trav - 'lin' down to
From Cal - i - for - nia to New Eng - land, down to
F♯dim7 C/G Cm/E♭ G/D G♯dim7
3fr
Dix - ie's sun - ny shore,
Dix - ie's sun - ny shore,
from At - lan - tic to Pa -

Am7
D7
G7
C♯dim7
Dm7
G7
cif - ic, gee, the traf - fic is ter - rif - ic. Oh, there's
C
C7
F
C
no place like home for the hol - i - days,
G
C
B7
B♭7♭5
5fr
A7
'cause no mat - ter how far a - way you
D7
D7♭5
G7
C
C7
roam, if you want to be

F
F♯dim7
C/G
F♯dim7
hap - py in a mil - lion ways, for the
G7
Dm7
1
G7
C
G13
3fr
hol - i - days you can't beat home, sweet home.
Oh, there's
2
G7
C♯dim7
Dm7
can't beat home,
Dm/G
G7♭9
C
sweet home.

I Believe in Father Christmas

Words and Music by
Greg Lake and Peter Sinfield

G/D D G/D D G/D D G/D D
peace on earth; But in-stead it just kept on rain - ing A veil of tears for the
sil - ent night; and they told me a fair - y sto - ry Till I be-lieved in the
G/D D Am7/D G/D D
Vir - gin birth. I re-mem - ber one Christ - mas morn - ing A
Is - rael - ite and I be-lieved in Fa - ther Christ - mas. And I
Am7/D G/D D A
win-ter's light and a dis - tant choir. And the peal of a bell and that
looked to the sky with ex - cit - ed eyes. Till I woke with a yawn in the

* *Excerpt from "Lieutenant Kijé" by Prokofieff included by permission of the Copyright Owners Boosey & Hawkes Music Publishers.*

3. I wish you a hopeful Christmas
I wish you a brave New Year
All anguish, pain and sadness
Leave your heart and let your road be clear.
They said there'd be snow at Christmas
They said there'd be peace on earth
Hallelujah Noel be it heaven or hell
The Christmas we get we deserve.

I Saw Mommy Kissing Santa Claus

Words and Music by
Tommie Connor

G7♯5 C Cdim7 C
creep down the stairs to have a peep; she
D7 G7 Fm/A♭
thought that I was tucked up in my bed - room fast a -
G7 G7♯5 C G7 C Am
sleep. Then I saw Mom - my tick - le
Em Am C Cmaj7
San - ta Claus, un - der - neath his

C7
F
A7/E
Dm
beard so snow - y white.
Oh, what a
F
B7
C
A7
laugh it would have been, if Dad - dy had on - ly
Dm7
G7
C
F/A
Fm/A♭
G7
seen Mom - my kiss - ing San - ta Claus last
1
C
E♭dim7
Dm7
G7
night.
2
C
Dm7
C6
night.
8vb

I Want a Hippopotamus for Christmas

(Hippo the Hero)

Words and Music by
John Rox

Don't want a doll, no dink - y Tink - er Toy, I
Mom
Pop
says a hip-po would eat me up, but then
C7/E
Gm/D
C7
F7
want a hip - po - pot - a - mus to play with and en - joy. I
Teach - er says a hip - po is a veg - e - tar - i - an. I
B♭
B♭6
B♭
want a hip - po - pot - a - mus for Christ - mas, I
want a hip - po - pot - a - mus for Christ - mas, the
F7
Fdim7
F7
don't think San - ta Claus would mind, do you? He
kind I saw last sum - mer in the zoo. We

won't have to use our dirt - y chim - ney
got a car with room for two in our two - car gar -
C7/E
Gm/D
C7
flue, just bring him through the front door, that's the
age. I'd feed him there and wash him there and
F7
B♭9
B♭7
eas - y thing to do.
give him his mas - sage.
I can see me now on
E♭
3fr
Cm7
3fr
Fm7
B♭9
Christ - mas morn - ing creep - ing down the

E♭
3fr
Cm7♭5
F7
stairs,
oh, what joy and what sur - prise when I
B♭
Gm7
C
B♭
F♯dim7
C7
o - pen up my eyes to see my hip - po he - ro
Cm7/F
8fr
Fdim7
F7
B♭
B♭6
stand - ing there.
I want a hip - po - pot - a - mus for
B♭
B♭6
Christ - mas,
on - ly a hip - po - pot - a - mus will

F7
Fdim7
F7
do.
No croc - o - diles or
No kan - ga - roos or
C7
Gm7
C7
rhi - noc - er - os - es,
duck - bill plat - y - pus - es,
I on - ly like
F7
C7
F7
hip - po - pot - a - mus - es, and hip - po - pot - a - mus - es like me,
1
B♭
Edim7
F7sus
F7
2
B♭
too.
I too.
sfz

I'll Be Home For Christmas

Words and Music by
Kim Gannon and Walter Kent

C
E♭dim7
Dm7
Gsus
3fr
G7
I'll be home for Christ - mas,
Em7♭5
A7
Dm7
G7
you can count on me.
Fm
G7♭9
Cmaj7
Am7
Please have snow and mis - tle - toe and
D7
A♭dim7
Dm7/G
G7
pres - ents on the tree.

C
E♭dim7
Dm7
Gsus
3fr
G7
Em7♭5
Christ - mas Eve will find me ___ where the
A7
Dm7
F6
Fm6
love - light gleams. ___ I'll be home for
Em
A7
D7
Dm7
G7♭9
Christ - mas, if on - ly in my
1
C
Dm7
G7♯5
dreams. ___
2
C
dreams. ___
rit.

It Must Have Been the Mistletoe
(Our First Christmas)

Words and Music by
Justin Wilde and Doug Konecky

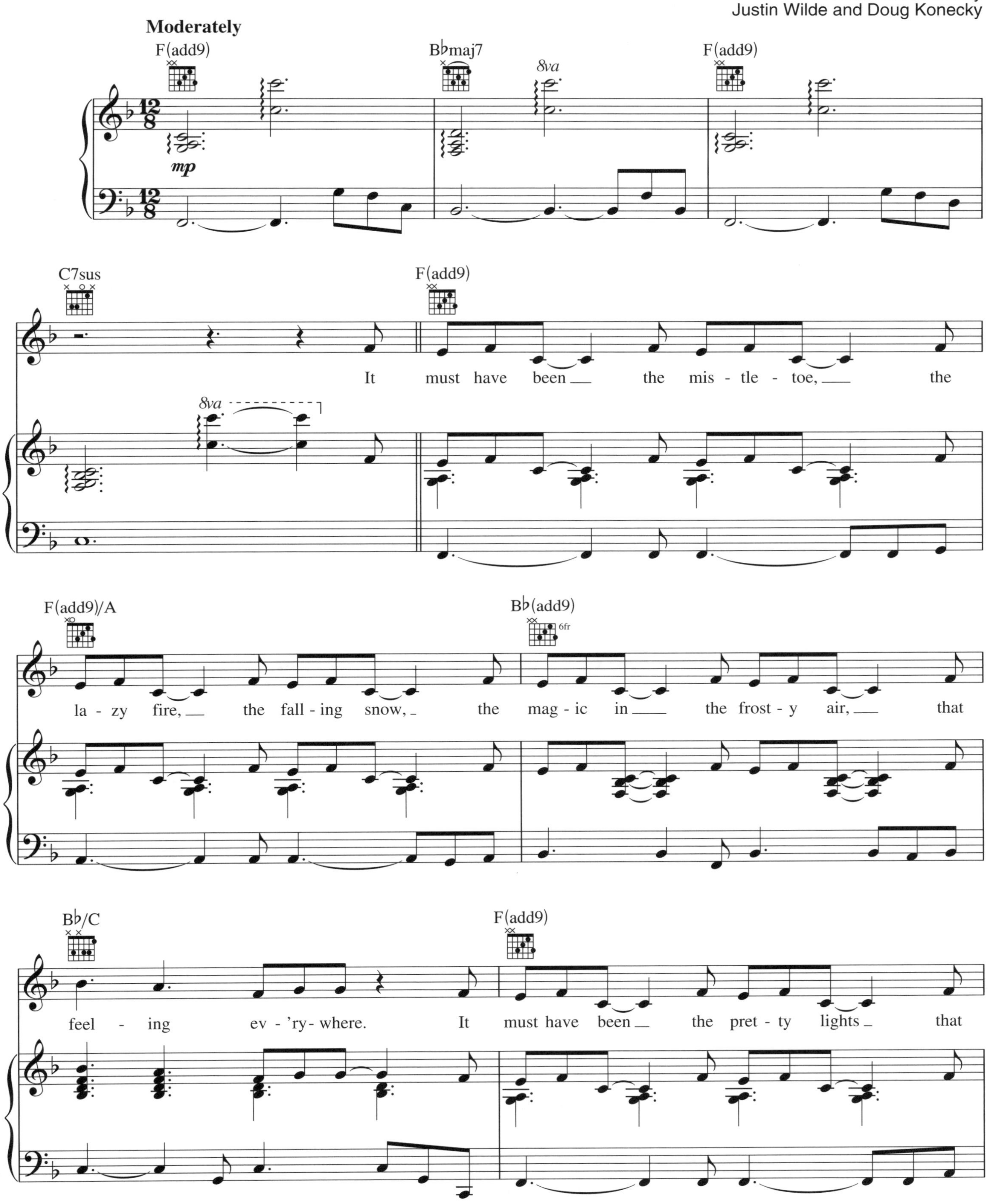

Moderately

F(add9) Bbmaj7 F(add9)

mp 8va

C7sus F(add9)

It must have been the mis - tle - toe, the

F(add9)/A Bb(add9)

la - zy fire, the fall - ing snow, the mag - ic in the frost - y air, that

Bb/C F(add9)

feel - ing ev - 'ry - where. It must have been the pret - ty lights that

Cm7
E♭/F
B♭maj7
Gm7
3fr
glis - tened _ in the si - lent night, _ or may - be just ___ the stars so bright _ that
B♭/C
B♭maj7
Fmaj7
shined a - bove you. Our first Christ - mas,
mf
Gm7
C9
Fmaj7
more than ___ we'd been dream - ing of. ___
B♭m7
E♭9
Cm7
Fm7
3fr
Old Saint Nich - 'las
f

B♭7sus
B♭7
B♭/C
C
B♭/C
had his fin - gers crossed that we would fall in love. It
F(add9)
F(add9)/A
could have been the hol - i - day, the mid-night ride up - on a sleigh, the
mp
B♭(add9)
6fr
B♭/C
coun - try - side all dressed in white, that cra - zy snow - ball fight. It
F(add9)
Cm7
3fr
E♭/F
could have been the stee - ple bell that wrapped us up with - in its spell. It

B♭maj7
Gm7
B♭/C
C6
on - ly took one kiss to know, it must have been the
F(add9)
B♭maj7
Fmaj7
mis-tle-toe. Our first Christ - mas,
mf
Gm7
C9
Fmaj7
more than we'd been dream - ing of.
B♭m7
E♭9
Cm7
3fr
Fm7
Old Saint Nich - 'las
f

B♭7sus
B♭7
D♭/E♭
must have known that kiss would lead to all of this. It
A♭(add9)
4fr
A♭(add9)/C
8fr
must have been the mis - tle - toe, the la - zy fire, the fall - ing snow, the
D♭(add9)
D♭/E♭
mag - ic in the frost - y air, that made me love you. On
A♭(add9)
4fr
E♭m7
6fr
G♭/A♭
Christ mas Eve a wish came true, that night I fell in love with you. It

D♭(add9)
B♭m7
D♭/E♭
on - ly took one kiss to know, it must have been the
A♭(add9)
A♭(add9)/C
4fr
8fr
B♭m7
E♭6
C/E
mis - tle - toe! It must have been the
mf rit.
Freely
Fm
Fm(maj7)
Fm7
Fm6
B♭m7
D♭/E♭
mis - tle - toe! It must have been the
mp
A♭(add9)
D♭maj7
A♭(add9)
mis - tle - toe!
8va
a tempo
rit.

It's Beginning to Look Like Christmas

By Meredith Willson

E♭/B♭
Edim7
B♭7
B♭m7/E♭
E♭7
can - dy canes and sil - ver lanes a - glow.
stur - dy kind that does - n't mind a snow.
It's be -
A♭
D♭
A♭
C7
gin-ning to look a lot like Christ - mas,
toys in ev - 'ry
soon the bells will
D♭
F7
B♭m7
Bdim
store. But the pret - ti - est sight to see is the
start. And the thing that will make them ring is the
A♭/C
A♭/G♭
F7
B♭m
E♭7
To Coda
hol - ly that will be on your own front
car - ol that you sing right with - in your

A♭
C7
door. A pair of hop - a - long boots and a pis - tol that shoots is the
Fm
C7
Fm
B♭7
wish of Bar - ney and Ben. Dolls that will talk and will go for a walk is the
E♭
B♭7
E♭
E♭7
hope of Jan - ice and Jen. And Mom and Dad can hard - ly wait for
Adim7
E♭7
D.S. al Coda
school to start a - gain. It's be -
CODA
A♭
heart.

Jingle Bells

Words and Music by
J. Pierpont

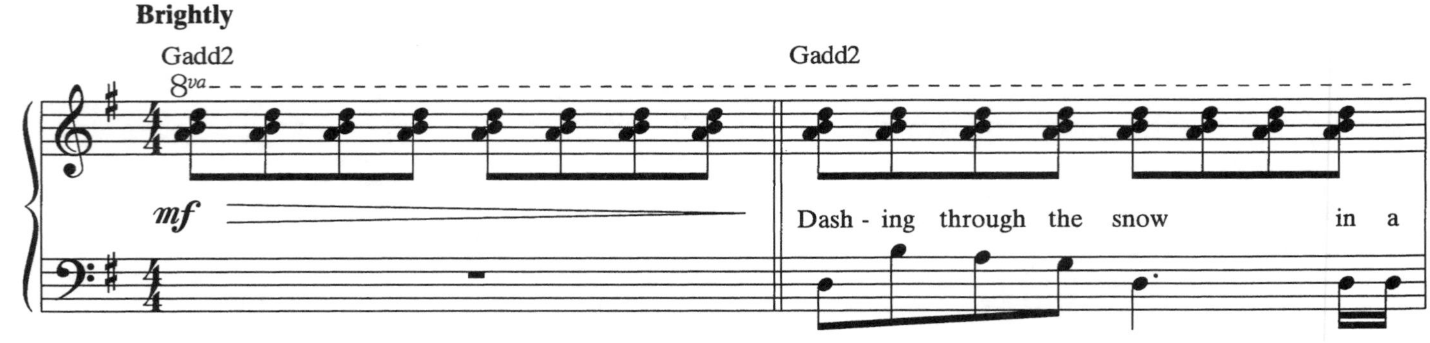

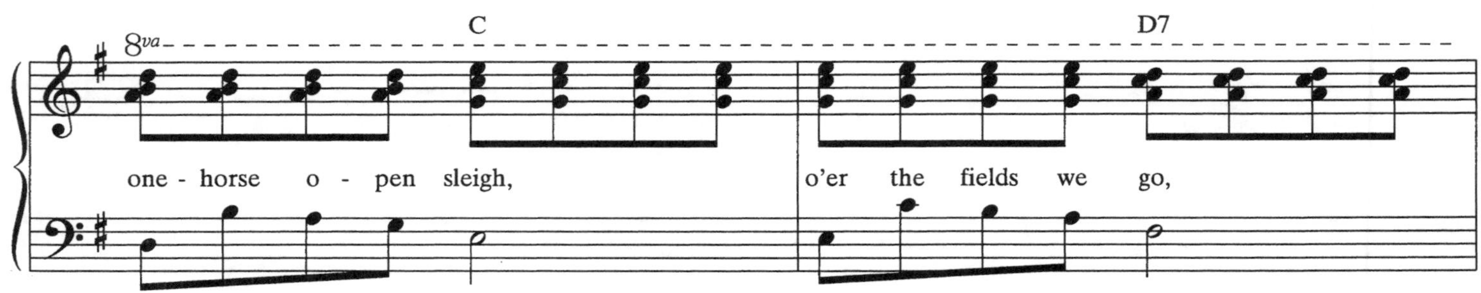

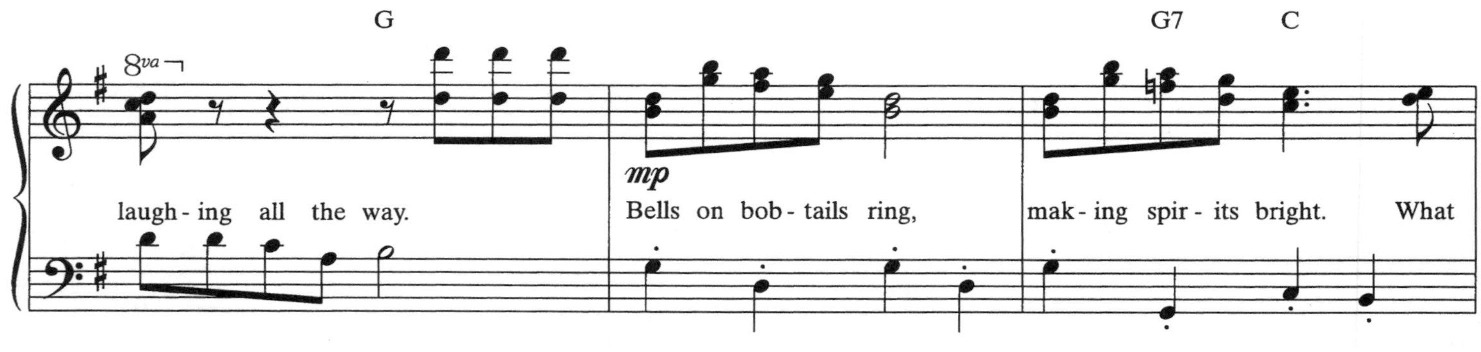

G
Jin - gle bells, jin - gle bells,
jin - gle all the way!

C Cm G
A7 D D7
Oh, what fun it is to ride in a
one - horse o - pen sleigh!

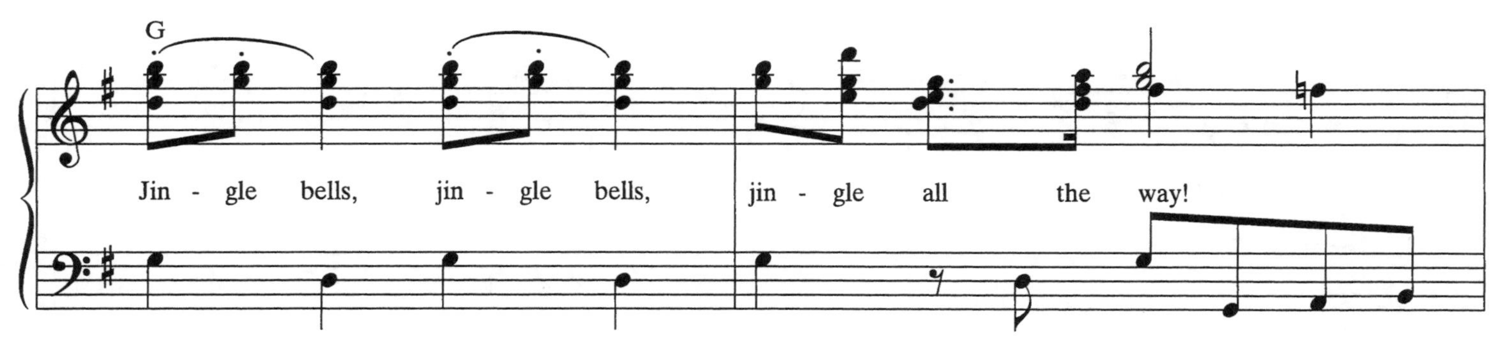
G
Jin - gle bells, jin - gle bells,
jin - gle all the way!

C Cm G
D7 G
Oh, what fun it is to ride in a
one - horse o - pen sleigh. Hey!

Joy to the World

Words by Isaac Watts

Music by George Frideric Handel
Adapted by Lowell Mason

2. Joy to the world! the Savior reigns.
Let men their songs employ
While fields and floods, rocks, hills and plains
Repeat the sounding joy, repeat the sounding joy,
Repeat, repeat the sounding joy.

3. No more let sin and sorrow grow,
Nor thorns infest the ground.
He comes to make His blessings flow
Far as the curse is found, far as the curse is found,
Far as, far as the curse is found.

4. He rules the world with truth and grace
And makes the nation prove
The glories of His righteousness
And wonders of His love, and wonders of His love,
And wonders, wonders of His love.

A Marshmallow World

Words by Carl Sigman

Music by Peter De Rose

C
marsh - mal - low clouds be - ing friend - ly in the arms of the ev - er - green
G7
Dm
G7
C
trees. And the sun is red like a pump - kin head. It's
D7
G7
C
Gm7
C7
shin - ing so your nose won't freeze. The world is your snow - ball,
F
Gm7
C7
F
see how it grows. That's how it goes, when - ev - er it snows. The

Am
D7
G
Em
Am
D7
world is your snow - ball, just for a song. Get out and roll it a -
G7
C
long. It's a yum, yum - my world made for sweet - hearts. Take a
G7
Dm
G7
walk with your fa - vor - ite girl. It's a sug - ar date, what if
Am
D7
Dm7
G7
C
spring is late. In win - ter it's a marsh - mal - low world.

Let It Snow! Let It Snow! Let It Snow!

Words by Sammy Cahn

Music by Jule Styne

F/A
A♭dim7
C7/G
D7/F♯
Gm
D7
Gm
A♭dim7
brought some corn for pop - ping. The lights are turned way down low;
dear, we're still good - bye - ing, but as long as you love me so,
Let it
C7
To Coda
F
C
C♯dim7
snow! Let it snow! Let it snow! When we fi - nal - ly kiss good - night, how I'll
Dm7
G7
C
B+
Gm/B♭
A7
hate go - ing out in the storm! But if you'll real - ly hold me tight,
D7
G7
C7
D.S. al Coda
all the way home I'll be warm. The
CODA
F
snow!

Little Saint Nick

Words and Music by
Brian Wilson and Mike Love

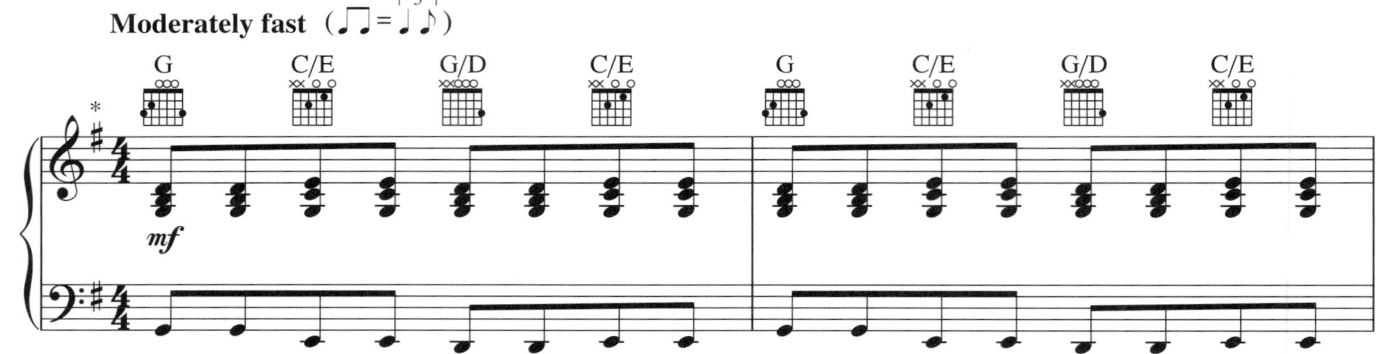

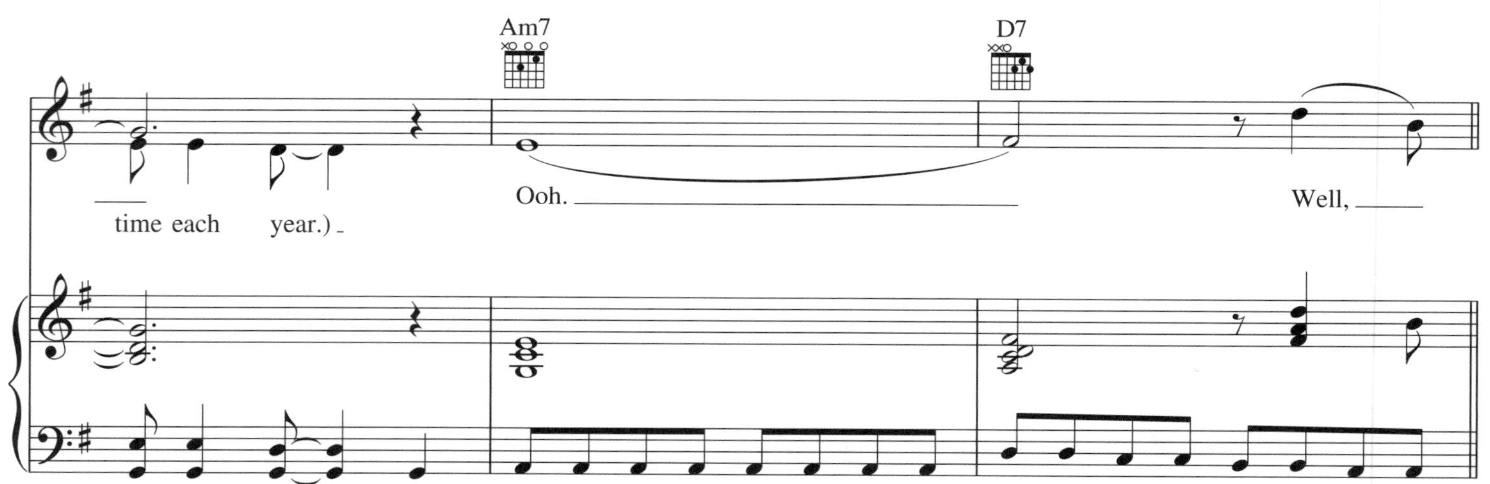

* *Recorded a half step lower.*

Am7
D7
Am7
D7
way up north where the air gets cold, there's a
lit - tle bob - sled, we call it Old Saint Nick, but she'll
haul - in' through the snow at a fright - 'nin' speed with a

G
Gmaj7
G6
G♯dim7
tale a - bout Chirst - mas that you've all been told. And a
walk a to - bog - gan with a four - speed stick. She's
half a doz - en deer with Ru - dy to lead. He's

Am7
D7
Am7
D7
real fa - mous cat all dressed up in red, and he
can - dy ap - ple red with a ski for a wheel, and when
got - ta wear his gog - gles 'cause the snow real - ly flies, and he's

G
Gmaj7
G6
G7
spends the whole year work - in' out on his sled.
San - ta hits the gas, man, just watch her peel.
cruis - in' ev - 'ry pad with a lit - tle sur - prise.
It's the
To Coda
C
Am7
Lit - tle Saint Nick. (Lit - tle Saint Nick.) It's the Lit - tle Saint Nick. (Lit - tle
1
D
2
D
C
F/C
C
Saint Nick.) Just a Saint Nick.) Run, run, rein - deer.
F
B♭/F
F
Run, run, rein - deer. Oh.

C
F/C
C
A
Run, run, rein - deer.
Run, run, rein - deer. He
N.C.
D.S. al Coda
don't miss no one. And
CODA
G
Lit - tle Saint Nick. (Lit - tle
E7/G♯
Am7
D7
Am7
D7
Saint Nick.) Ah,
Mer - ry Christ-mas, Saint
Repeat and Fade
G
E7/G♯
3
Nick.
(Christ - mas comes this time each year.)
Ah,
Optional Ending
G
Nick.

The Marvelous Toy

Words and Music by
Tom Paxton

D7
G7
C
gave to me a toy. A won - der to be -
looked like big green eyes. I first pushed one and
was - n't e - ven there! I start - ed to sob and my
mar - v'lous lit - tle toy. His eyes near - ly popped right
G7
C
F
hold it was, with man - y col - ors bright, And the
then the oth - er, and then I twist - ed its lid, And
dad - dy laughed, For he knew that I would find, When I
out of his head, And he gave a squeal of glee, Nei - ther
C
Am
D7
G7
mo - ment I laid eyes on it, it be - came my heart's de - light.
when I set it down a - gain here is what it did:
turned a - round, my mar - vel - ous toy chug - gin' from be - hind.
one of us knows just what it is but he loves it just like me.

G7
C
G7
It went "Zip" when it moved, And "Bop" when it stopped, And
It still goes "Zip" when it moves, And "Bop" when it stops, And
C
F
"Whirr" when it stood still, I nev - er knew just
"Whirr" when it stands still, I nev - er knew just
C
G7
1.2.3.4.
C
G7
what it was and I guess I nev - er will. The
what it was and I guess I nev - er will. It
Well the
5.
C
G7
C
will.
3

Merry Christmas, Darling

Words and Music by
Richard Carpenter and Frank Pooler

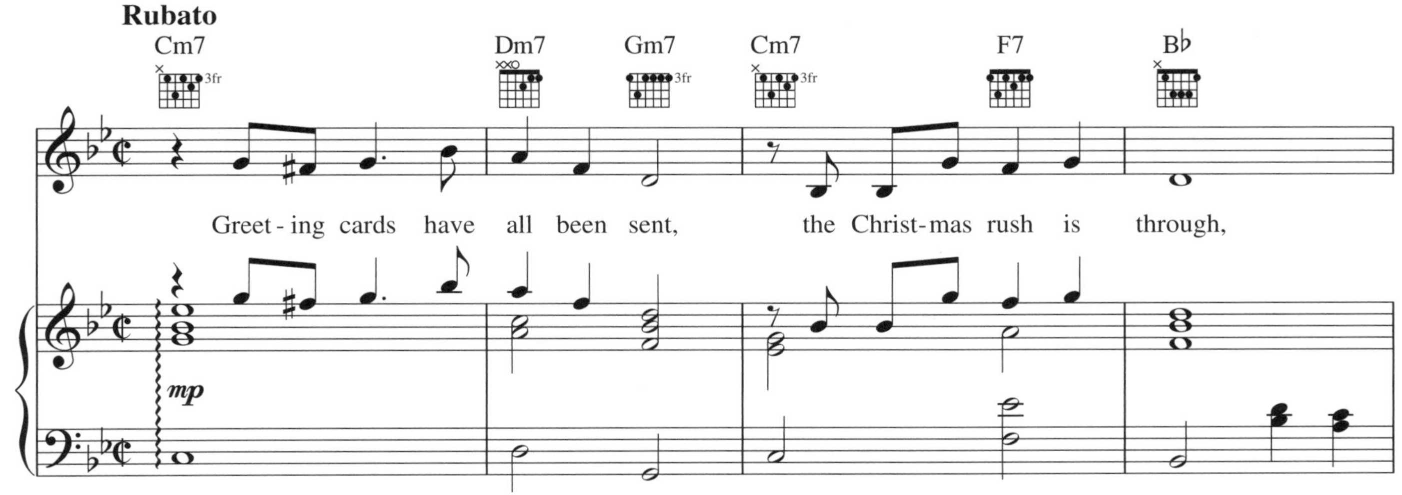

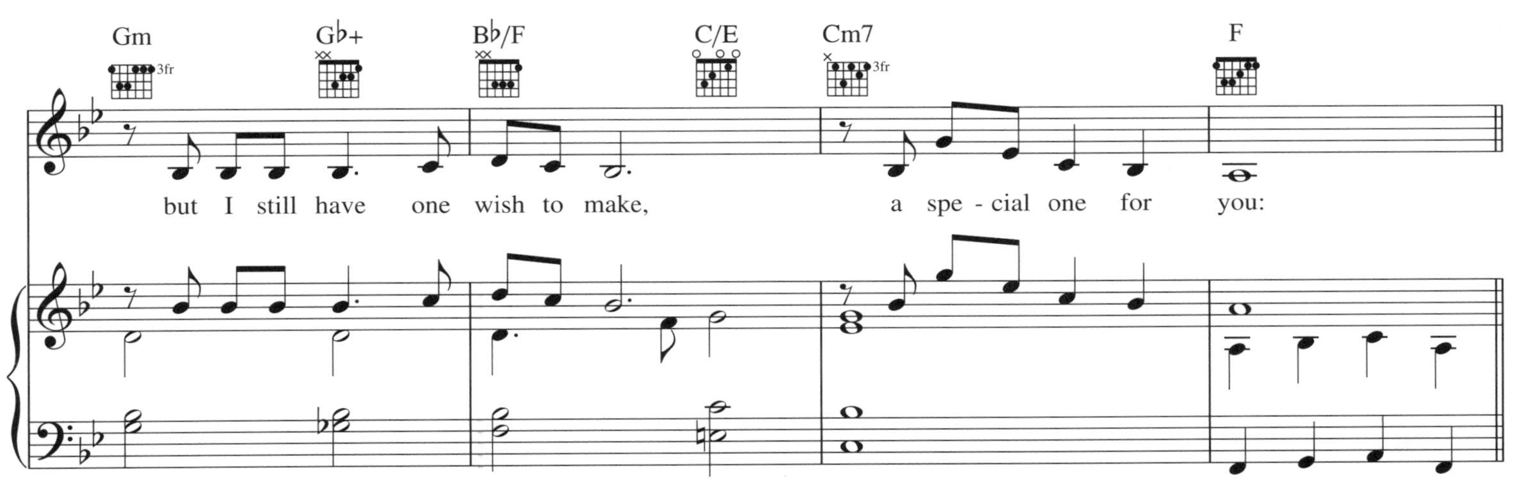

E♭ F/E♭ Dm7 Gm7 Cm7 Dm E♭6 E♭/F F7
3fr 3fr 3fr
I can dream and in my dreams, I'm Christ - mas - ing with you.
B♭maj9 Cm/B♭ B♭maj9 Fm7 A♭/B♭
4fr
Hol - i - days are joy - ful, there's al - ways some - thing new. But
E♭ F/E♭ Dm7 Gm7 C/E E♭m6 A♭7
3fr 3fr 4fr
ev - 'ry day's a hol - i - day when I'm near to you. The
D♭ E♭/D♭ Cm7 Fm B♭m7 E♭7 A♭
3fr 3fr 4fr
lights on my tree I wish you could see, I wish it ev - 'ry day. The

Fm
Fm(maj7)
Fm7
F7
B♭
Cm
Dm
Cm7
F
logs on the fire fill me with de - sire to see you and to say that I
B♭maj9
Cm/B♭
B♭maj9
Fm7
E7♭5
wish you mer - ry Christ - mas, hap - py New Year too. I've
To Coda
E♭
F/E♭
Dm7
Gm7
Cm7
F7
B♭
A♭7
D.S. al Coda
just one wish on this Christ - mas Eve: I wish I were with you. The
CODA
Cm7
F
E♭
Dm7♭5
G7
Cm7
F7
B♭
I wish I were with you, I wish I were with you.
rit.

Mistletoe and Holly

Words and Music by Frank Sinatra,
Dok Stanford and Henry W. Sanicola

E♭m7
A♭7
D♭maj7
D♭6
E♭m7
A♭7
D♭maj7
D♭6
Then comes that big night, giv - ing the tree the trim,
Am7
D7
Gmaj7
G6/D
Gm7
C9
F7
D.C. al Coda
you'll hear voic - es by star - light sing - ing a yule - tide hymn.
CODA
Cm7
F7
D7♯5
G7
C7
folks steal in' a kiss or two as they whis - per, "Mer - ry
F7
B♭
Cm7
F7
B♭
Christ - mas to you."

The Most Wonderful Time of the Year

Words and Music by
Eddie Pola and George Wyle

Bm7
E7
C♯m7
4fr
with the kids jin - gle - bell - ing and ev - 'ry - one
with those hol - i - day greet - ings and gay hap - py
There'll be much mis - tle - toe - ing and hearts will be
F♯m7
Bm7
A/C♯
D
D♯dim7
To Coda
tell - ing you, "Be of good cheer."
meet - ings, when friends come to call.
glow - ing when loved ones are near.
It's the
It's the
It's the
1
A/E
D/E
A
F♯m7
most won - der - ful time of the year.
Bm7
D/E
2
C♯m7
4fr
F♯m7
Bm7
E7
It's the hap - hap - pi - est sea - son of

Em7
A7
D/A
all. There'll be par - ties for
Bm7
C♯m7
4fr
F♯m7
Bm7
E7
host - ing, marsh - mal - lows for toast - ing and car - ol - ing out in the
A
Dm7
G7
Cmaj7
snow. There'll be scar - y ghost sto - ries and tales of the
Fmaj7
Dm
Bm7♭5
D/E
E7
D.S. al Coda
glo - ries of Christ - mas - es long, long a - go. It's the

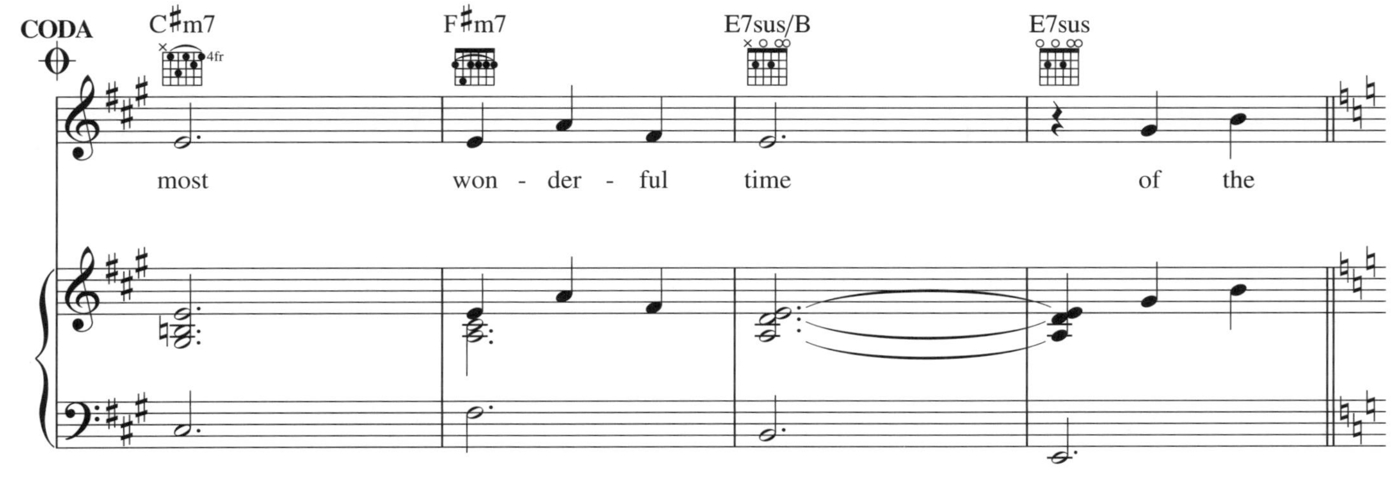
CODA
C♯m7
4fr
F♯m7
E7sus/B
E7sus
most
won - der - ful
time
of
the

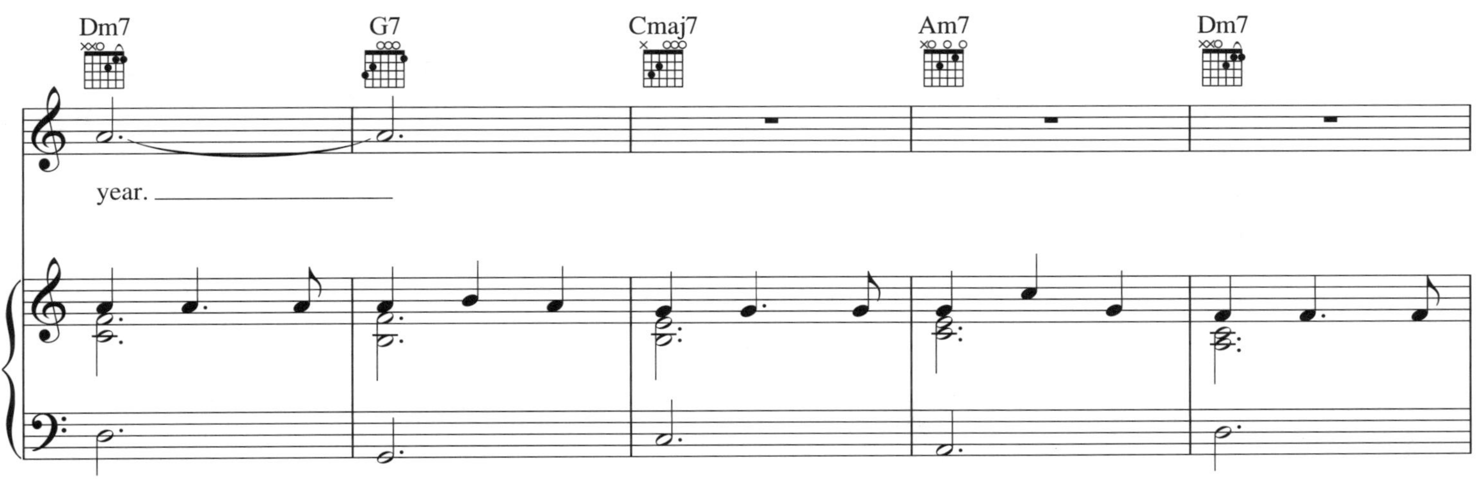
Dm7
G7
Cmaj7
Am7
Dm7
year.

G7
Cmaj7
Cm7
3fr
F7

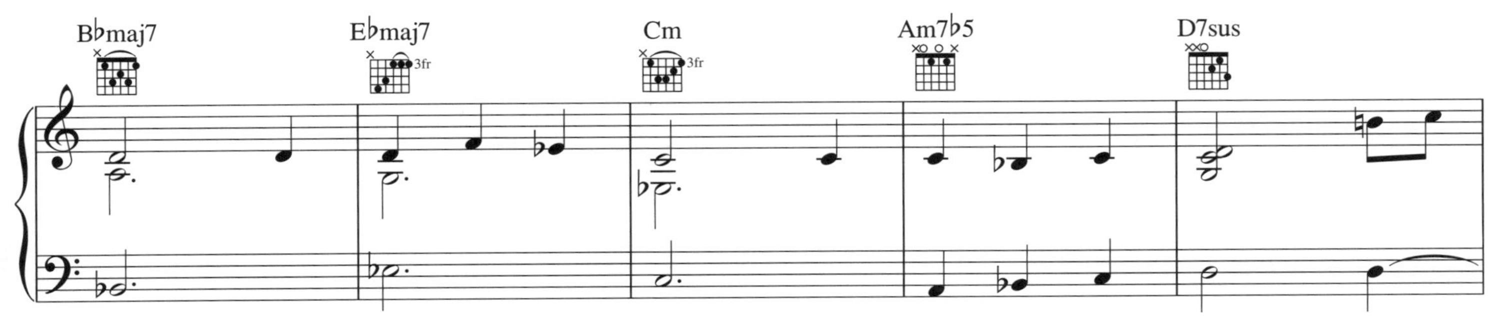
B♭maj7
E♭maj7
3fr
Cm
3fr
Am7♭5
D7sus

Em7
F9sus
B♭/F
F7sus
It's the most won - der - ful time of the
B♭/F
F7sus
Cm7
F7
3fr
year.
There'll be much mis - tle - toe - ing and
Dm7
G7
Cm7
3fr
hearts will be glow - ing when loved ones are near.

A7
B♭/F
F7sus
B♭/F
It's the most won - der - ful time, it's the most
F7sus
B♭/F
won - der - ful time, it's the most won - der - ful
F7sus
E♭
3fr
F
B♭
time of the year.
C♭(♭5)
Fm7
F7/B
B♭
F7
B♭

My Favorite Things

from THE SOUND OF MUSIC

Lyrics by Oscar Hammerstein II

Music by Richard Rodgers

Em
Cream col - ored pon - ies and crisp ap - ple
mf
mp
Cmaj7
strud - els, Door - bells and sleigh - bells and schnitz - el with noo - dles,
Am7
D7
G/B
C/E
G/D
Wild geese that fly with the moon on their wings, These are a
C
F♯m7♭5
4fr
B7
E
few of my fa - vor - ite things.
f

A
Girls in white dress - es with blue sat - in sash - es, Snow - flakes that
mf
Am7
D7
stay on my nose and eye - lash - es, Sil - ver white win - ters that
G/B
C/E
G/D
C
F♯m7♭5
4fr
B7♭9
melt in - to springs, These are a few of my fa - vor - ite things.
Em
F♯m7♭5
4fr
B7
When the dog bites, When the bee stings,
mf

Em
C
When I'm feel - ing sad, I
A7/C#
A7
sim - ply re - mem - ber my fa - vor - ite things and
G/D C/D G/D C/D G D7♭9 D7 G
4fr
then I don't feel so bad.
cresc.
f
C G/D D7 G
sf

Nuttin' for Christmas

Words and Music by
Roy C. Bennett and Sid Tepper

G7 C7 F Gm7 F/A Gm7 F F#dim7
some - bod - y snitched on me. I spilled some ink on
some - bod - y snitched on me. I did a dance on
some - bod - y snitched on me. Next year I'll be
Gm7 Gb7 Gm7 C7b9 Fmaj7 Dm7
Mom - my's rug, I made Tom - my eat a bug,
Mom - my's plants, climbed a tree and tore my pants,
go - ing straight, next year I'll be good, just wait.
Bb F/A Gm7 C7
bought some gum with a pen - ny slug; some - bod - y snitched on
filled the sug - ar bowl with ants; some - bod - y snitched on
I'd start now but ___ it's too late; some - bod - y snitched on
F6 C9#5 F Am/E
me. Oh,
me. So,
me. Oh,
I'm get - tin' nut - tin' for

Dm7
F/C
Gm
3fr
Christ - mas.
Mom - my and
G/F
C9/E
Dad - dy are mad.
F
Am/E
Dm7
I'm get - tin' nut - tin' for Christ - mas,
F/C
Gm7
C7♭9
'cause I ain't been nut - tin' but

1, 2
F6
Gm7
C7
3
F6
bad.
(1., 2.) I
bad.
Gm7
C7
F
D7
So you bet - ter be good, what - ev - er you do, 'cause
Gm7
C7
Am7
D7
Gm7
if you're bad, I'm warn - ing you, you'll get
C7
F6
nut - tin' for Christ - mas.

O Come, All Ye Faithful
(Adeste Fideles)

Latin Words translated by Frederick Oakeley

Music by John Francis Wade

G/B
D7/A
G
D7sus4/A
D7/A
G
D/F♯
G
Em
Am/C
Come and be - hold him, born the King of
Glo - ry to God in the

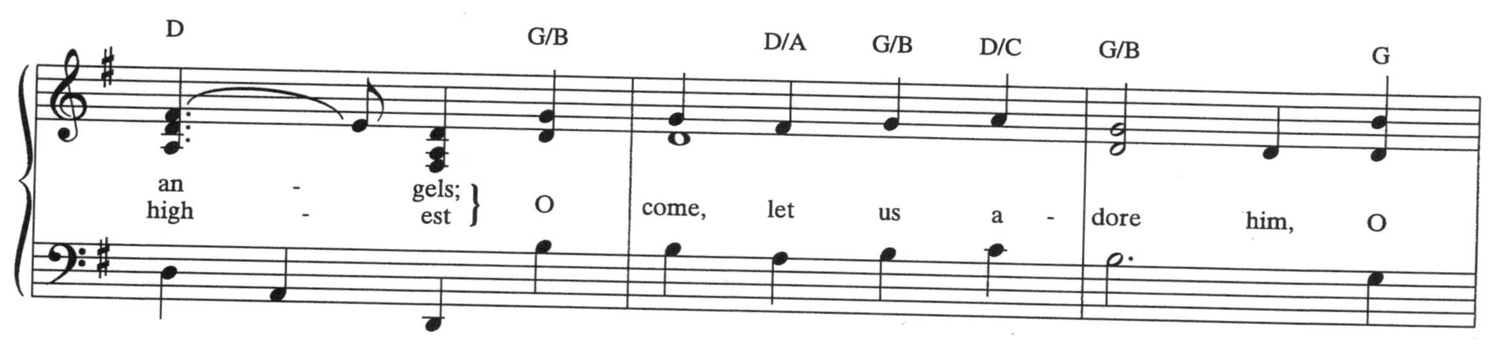
D
G/B
D/A
G/B
D/C
G/B
G
an - gels;
high - est
O come, let us a - dore him, O

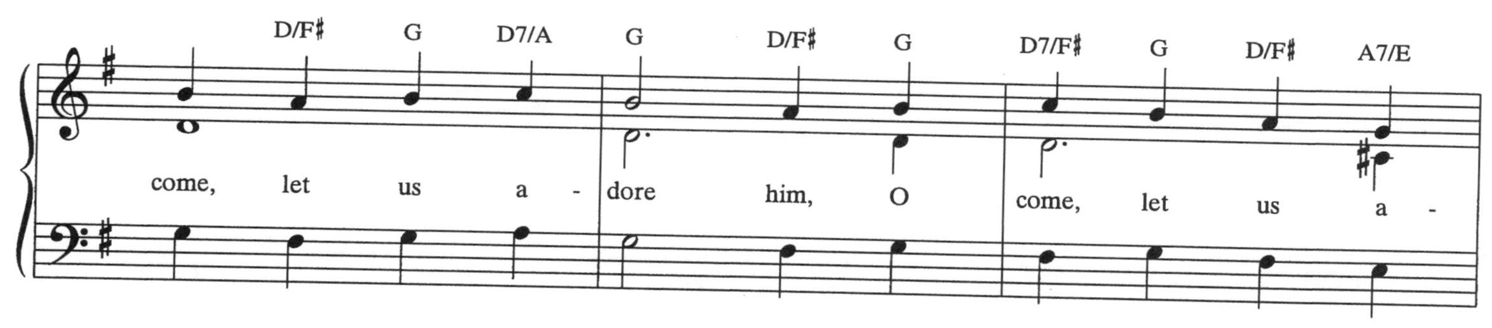
D/F♯
G
D7/A
G
D/F♯
G
D7/F♯
G
D/F♯
A7/E
come, let us a - dore him, O come, let us a -

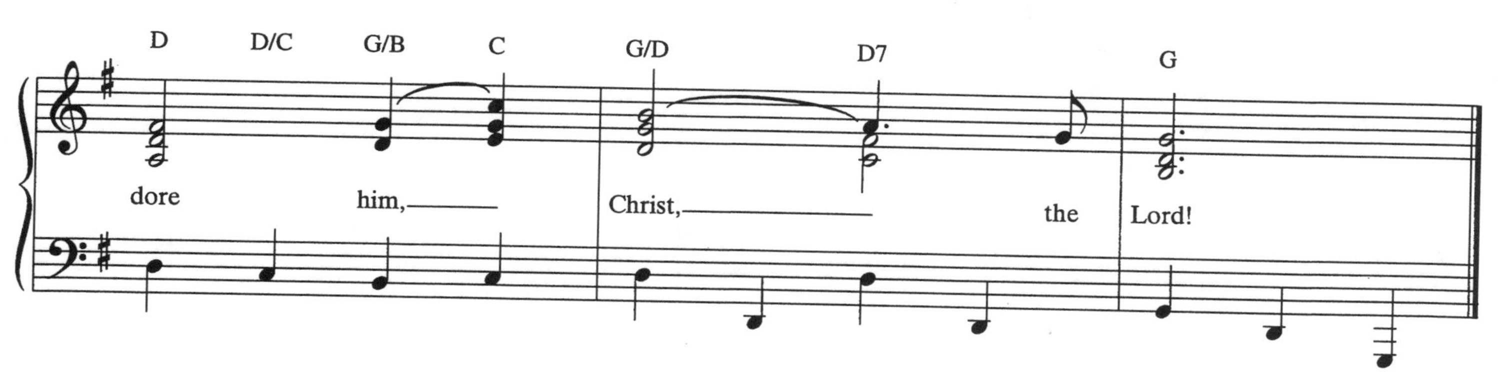
D
D/C
G/B
C
G/D
D7
G
dore him, Christ, the Lord!

O Little Town of Bethlehem

Words by Phillips Brooks

Music by Lewis H. Redner

F/E♭ D Gm F/C C7
bove thy deep and dream - less sleep The si - lent stars go
mor - tals sleep the an - gels keep Their watch of won - d'ring
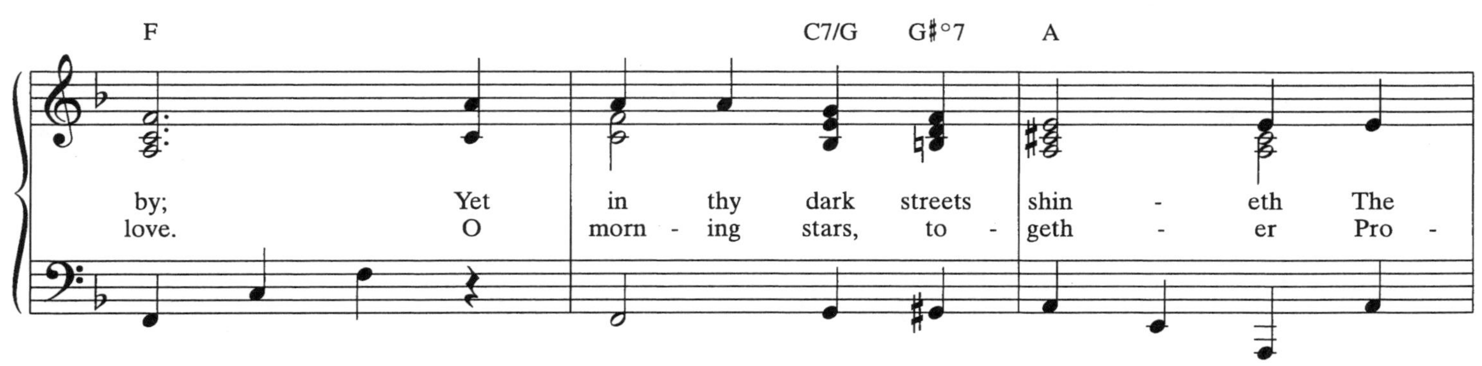
F C7/G G♯°7 A
by; Yet in thy dark streets shin - eth The
love. O morn - ing stars, to - geth - er Pro -
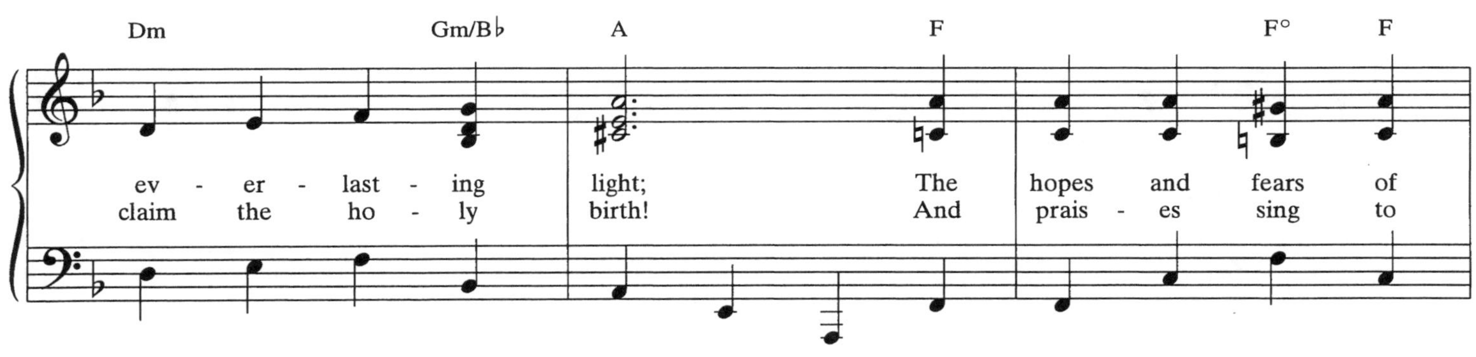
Dm Gm/B♭ A F F° F
ev - er - last - ing light; The hopes and fears of
claim the ho - ly birth! And prais - es sing to
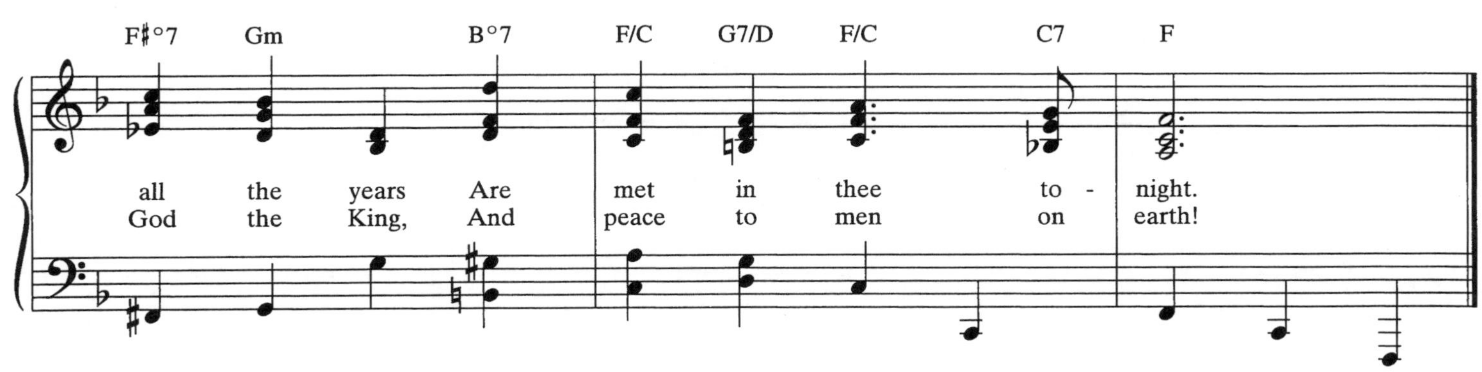
F♯°7 Gm B°7 F/C G7/D F/C C7 F
all the years Are met in thee to - night.
God the King, And peace to men on earth!

Please Come Home for Christmas

Words and Music by
Charles Brown and Gene Redd

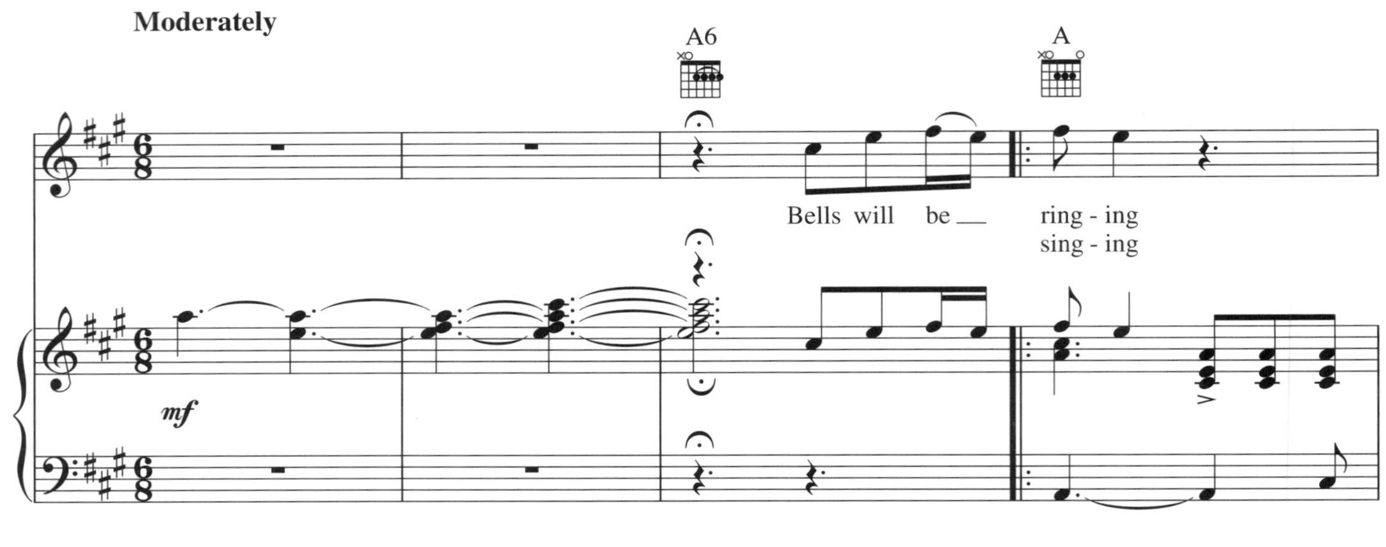

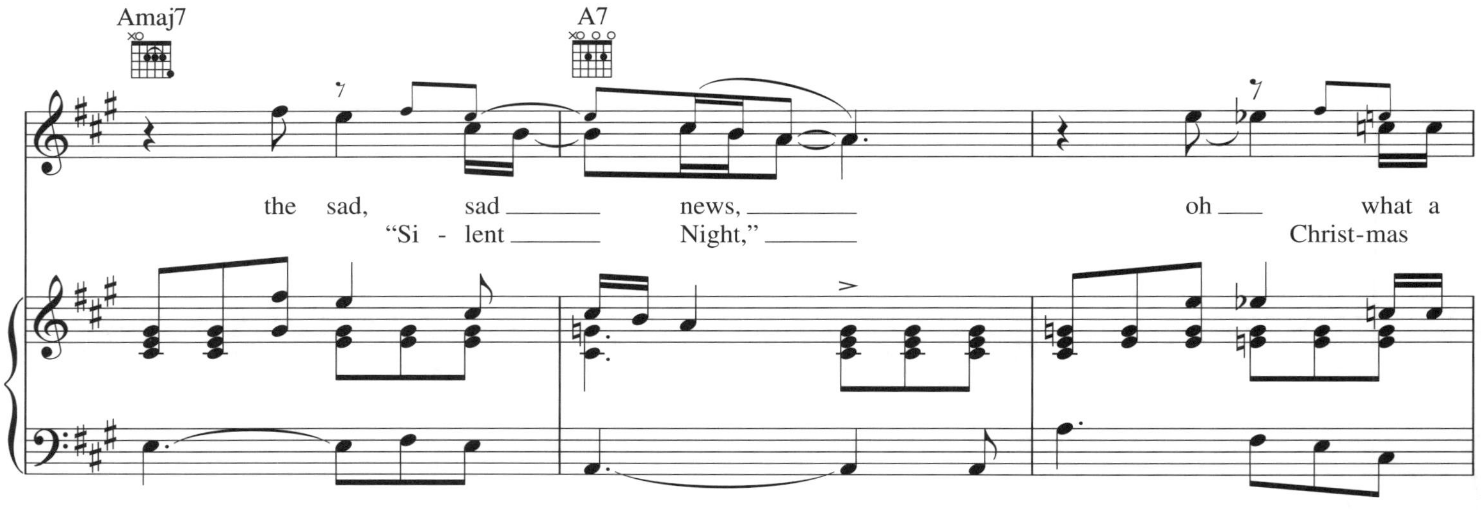

A
D
My ba - by's gone.
Please come home for Christ-mas,
I have no
please come home for
A
A/G♯
F♯m7
B7
friends
Christ-mas;
to wish me greet-ings
if not for Christ-mas,
1
E7
E7♯5
once a - gain.
Choirs will be
2
E7
A
A7
by New Year's night.
Friends and re -

D
Dm
la - tions
send sal - u - ta - tions
A
E7#5
sure as the stars shine a - bove
A
A7
D
For this is Christ - mas,
Dm
yes, Christ - mas my dear,
it's the time of

B7
E7
year to be with the one you love.
E7♯5
A
Amaj7
So won't you tell me you'll nev-er-more
(Instrumental)
A7
D
roam. Christ-mas and New Year
D♯dim
6fr
will find you home.
(Instrumental ends) Ooo
There'll be no more

A
C♯7
F♯m
A/E
sor - row
no grief and pain
D♯dim
6fr
B7/D♯
A/E
F♯m7
1
B7
E7
and I'll be
hap - py,
hap - py.
hap - py
once a -
A
E7♯5
2
B7
E7
gain.
Christ - mas
once a -
A
D/A
A
gain.

Pretty Paper

Words and Music by
Willie Nelson

D7 G G/D G
by. Should you stop? Bet-ter not, much too bus - y.
D7 G
You're in a hur - ry; my, how time does fly. In the
G7 C G
dis - tance the ring - ing of laugh - ter, and in the midst of the
D7 G
laugh - ter he cries: Pret - ty pa - per, pret - ty rib - bons of

D7
blue. Wrap your pres - ents to your dar - ling from
G G7 C
you. Pret - ty pen - cils to write, "I love you."
G D7 C G
Pret - ty pa - per, pret - ty rib - bons of blue. Pret - ty
1
2
G(add2)
blue.
decresc.
rit.
pp

Rockin' Around the Christmas Tree

Music and Lyrics by
Johnny Marks

G7
Christ - mas tree, let the Christ - mas spir - it ring.
Lat - er we'll have some pun - kin pie and we'll do some car - ol -
C
F
Em
ing. You will get a sen - ti - men - tal feel - ing when you
Am
Am(maj7)
Am7
D7
hear voic - es sing - ing, "Let's be jol - ly, deck the halls with

G7
C
boughs of hol - ly." Rock - in' a - round the Christ - mas tree, have a
G7
hap - py hol - i - day. Ev - 'ry - one danc - ing mer - ri - ly in the
1
Dm7/G
G7
C
new old - fash - ioned way.
2
Dm7/G
G7
new old - fash - ioned
C
way.

Rudolph the Red-Nosed Reindeer

Music and Lyrics by
Johnny Marks

A tempo
C
C/E
E♭dim7
Ru - dolph the red - nosed rein - deer had a ver - y shin - y
G7
nose, and if you ev - er saw it,
G7♯5
C
you would e - ven say it glows. All of the oth - er
C/E
E♭dim7
G7
rein - deer used to laugh and call him names.

They nev - er let poor Ru - dolph join in an - y rein - deer
C C7 F C Cmaj7
games. Then one fog - gy Christ - mas Eve,
Dm G7 C C#dim7 G/D
San - ta came to say, "Ru - dolph, with your
Gmaj7 G#dim7 Am7 D7 G7
nose so bright, won't you guide my sleigh to - night?"

C
C/E
E♭dim7
Then how the rein - deer loved him, as they shout - ed out with
G7
glee: "Ru - dolph the red - nosed rein - deer,
1
C
G9
9fr
G7♭9
you'll go down in his - to - ry!"
2
G7/D
C♯dim7
you'll go down in
G7/D
G7
C
Dm7
G7
C
his - to - ry!"

Santa Baby

By Joan Javits,
Phil Springer and Tony Springer

G
Em
A7
D7
G
Em
for me.
Been an aw-ful good girl,
San-ta Ba-by, so
the deed
to a plat-i-num mine,
San-ta hon-ey, so
Am
D7
G
Em
Am7
D7
hur-ry down the chim-ney to-night.
hur-ry down the chim-ney to-night.
3
3
G
Em
A7
D7
G
Em
San-ta Ba-by, a fif-ty-four con-vert-i-ble, too, light blue.
San-ta cu-tie, and fill my stock-ing with a du-plex and cheques.
A7
D7
G
Em
Am7
D7
I'll wait up for you, dear
San-ta Ba-by, so hur-ry down the chim-ney to-night.
Sign your X on the line,
San-ta cu-tie, and hur-ry down the chim-ney to-night.

G
Em
Am7
D7
G
B7
F♯m7/B
Think of all the
Come and trim my
B7
E7
Bm7/F♯
fun I've missed. Think of all the fel - las that I
Christ - mas tree with some dec - o - ra - tions bought at
E7
A7
Em7/A
have - n't kissed. Next year I could be
Tif - fa - ny. I real - ly do be -
A7
D
C♯
Am7/D
Edim7
D7
just as good if you check off my Christ - mas list.
lieve in you. Let's see if you be - lieve in me.

G Em A7 D7
San - ta Ba - by, I want a yacht and real - ly that's not
San - ta Ba - by, for - got to men - tion one lit - tle thing,
G Em A7 D7 G Em
a lot. Been an an - gel all year, San - ta Ba - by, so
a ring! I don't mean on your phone, San - ta Ba - by, so
Am7 D7
hur - ry down the chim - ney to - night.
hur - ry down the chim - ney to - night.
1 G Em
Am7 D7
2 G Em Am7 D7♭9 G6/9
4fr
3
3

Santa Claus Is Comin' to Town

Words by Haven Gillespie

Music by J. Fred Coots

C
C7
F
Fm6
C
C7
mak - ing a list and check - ing it twice, gon - na find out who's
F
Fm6
C
Am
Dm7
G7
naugh - ty and nice. San - ta Claus is com - in' to
C
C7
Gm7
C7
F
Dm7
town. He sees you when you're sleep - in'. He
Gm7
C7
F
Dm7
Am7
D7
knows when you're a - wake. He knows if you've been

G
E7
Am7
D7♭5
G
G7♯5
bad or good, so be good for good - ness sake. Oh! You
C
C7
F
Fm6
C
C7
bet - ter watch out, you bet - ter not cry, bet - ter not pout, I'm
F
Fm6
C
Am
Dm
G7
tell - ing you why: San - ta Claus is com - in' to
1
2
C
Am7
Dm7
G13
3fr
C
Fm6
C
town. You town.
3
3

Shake Me I Rattle
(Squeeze Me I Cry)

Words and Music by
Hal Hackady and Charles Naylor

E♭
look - ing at a dol - ly in a dress of ros - y
mem - bered, I re - mem - bered how I longed to make it
clos - ing up the toy shop as I hur - ried through the
Cm
C♯dim7
B♭
red and a - round the pret - ty dol - ly hung a
mine and a - round that oth - er dol - ly hung an -
door, just in time to buy the dol - ly that her
F7
B♭
lit - tle sign that said:
oth - er lit - tle sign:
heart was long - ing for.
Shake me, I
B♭+
E♭6
Cm
rat - tle; squeeze me, I cry.
As I
I had
And I

F7
F9
B♭
stood there be - side her I could hear her
count - ed my pen - nies Just a pen - my
gave her the dol - ly that we both had longed to
B♭6
B♭
B♭+
sigh.
shy.
buy.
Shake me, I rat - tle;
E♭6
Cm
3fr
F7
E♭6
squeeze me, I cry. Please take me
F7
B♭
1, 2
B♭
3
B♭
home and love me.
I re -
It was

Snowfall

Words and Music by
Ingrid Michaelson

C
G7
C
I'm a snow - fall kind of girl.
C
C7/E
F
Fm
I want a snow - fall kind of love that
C
G
G7
lights up the sky from be - low. Ooh.
C
C7/E
F
Fm
I want a snow - fall kind of love that
3

C
G7
C
brings people to their win - dow. Won't you
G
F
C
bur - y me in your qui - et love. Oh,
(mp, mf)
G
F
C
bur - y me in your qui - et love. Oh,
G
F
To Coda
Am
bur - y me in your qui - et love and

N.C.
C
C7/E
F
we will blow a - way.
mf
Fm
C
G7
C
C
C7/E
F
Fm
I want a snow - fall kind of love, the
3
C
G
G7
kind of love that keeps you in bed all day. Oh,

C
C7/E
F
Fm
I want to walk through with you and
C
G7
C
D.S. al Coda
watch it all melt a - way. Won't you
Coda
Am
F
G
C
and we will blow a - way.
(Mm, mm,
mp
F
Fm
C
G7
C
mm, mm, mm, mm, mm.)

Silent Night

Words by Joseph Mohr
Translated by John F. Young

Music by Franz X. Gruber

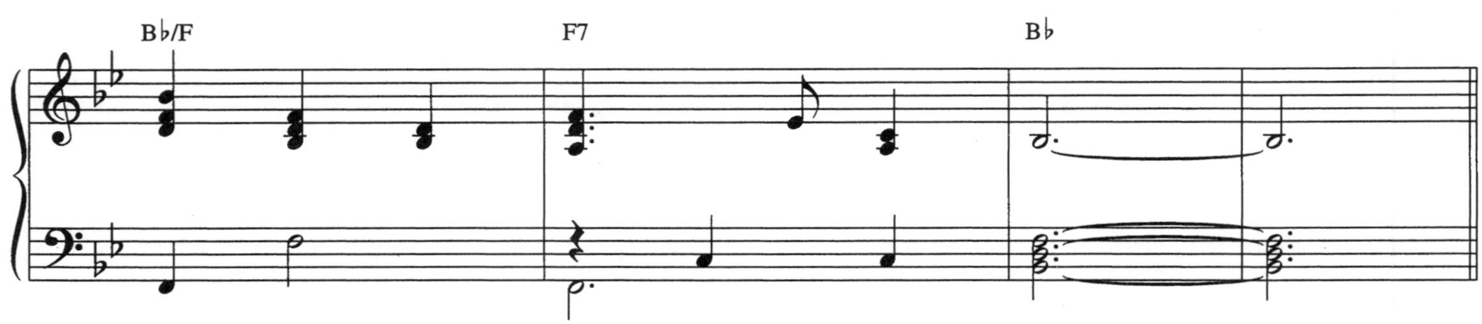

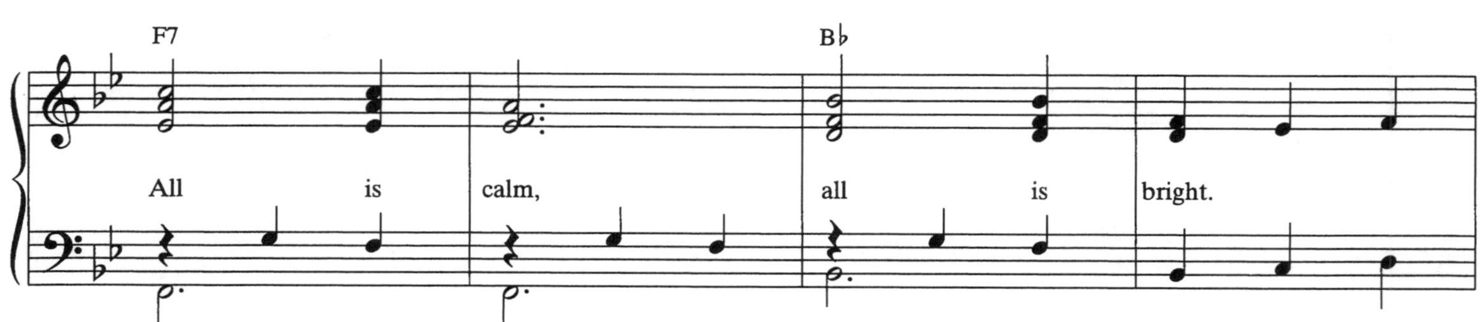

2. Silent night! Holy night! Shepherds quake at the sight!
Glories stream from heaven afar; heavenly hosts sing, "Alleluia!"
Christ, the Savior, is born! Christ, the Savior, is born!

3. Silent night! Holy night! Son of God, love's pure light!
Radiant beams from Thy holy face with the dawn of redeeming grace,
Jesus, Lord, at Thy birth! Jesus, Lord, at Thy birth!

Silver Bells

from the Paramount Picture THE LEMON DROP KID

Words and Music by
Jay Livingston and Ray Evans

C7
B♭/D
D♭dim7
F7/C
C7♭9
be, here is what Christ - mas - time means to
mp
rall.
Cm7/F
F7
B♭
B♭maj7
B♭7
E♭
me. Cit - y side - walks, bus - y side - walks dressed in hol - i - day
street lights, e - ven stop - lights blink a bright red and
E♭6
F7
B♭
style; in the air there's a feel - ing of Christ - mas.
green as the shop - pers rush home with their treas - ures.
E♭
B♭/D
Cm7/F
B♭
B♭maj7
B♭7
Chil - dren laugh - ing, peo - ple pass - ing, meet - ing
Hear the snow crunch, see the kids bunch, this is

E♭
E♭6
F7
3fr
smile af - ter smile, and on ev - 'ry street cor - ner you
San - ta's big scene, and a - bove all this bus - tle you
B♭
hear:
hear:
Sil - ver bells,
E♭
F
C7
sil - ver bells,
it's Christ - mas -
F7
B♭
time in the cit - y.

E♭
3fr
Ring - a - ling,
hear them ring,
F
C7
F7
soon it will be Christ - mas
1
B♭
E♭/B♭
6fr
B♭maj7
Cm/B♭
8fr
F13
Day.
Strings of
2
B♭
E♭/B♭
6fr
B♭maj7
F7
B♭
Day.
rall.

Star of Bethlehem

from the Twentieth Century Fox Feature Film HOME ALONE

Words by Leslie Bricusse

Music by John Williams

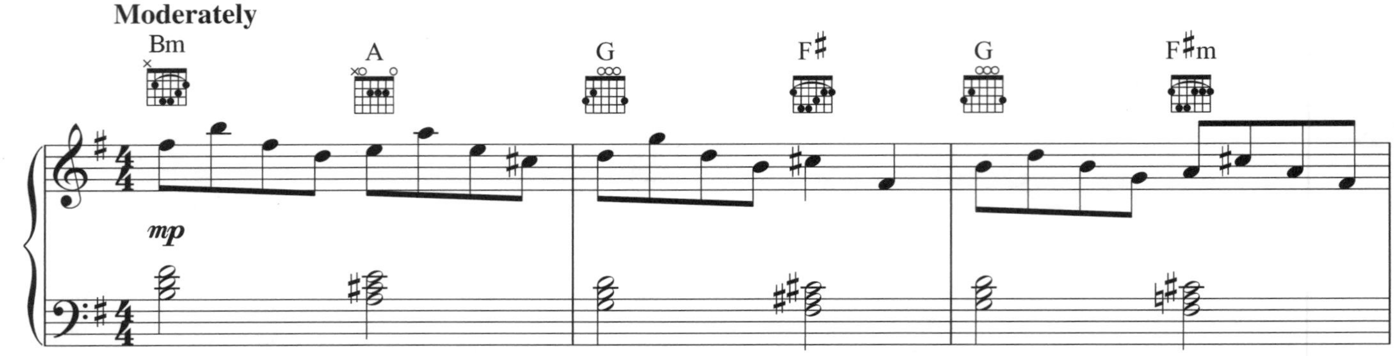

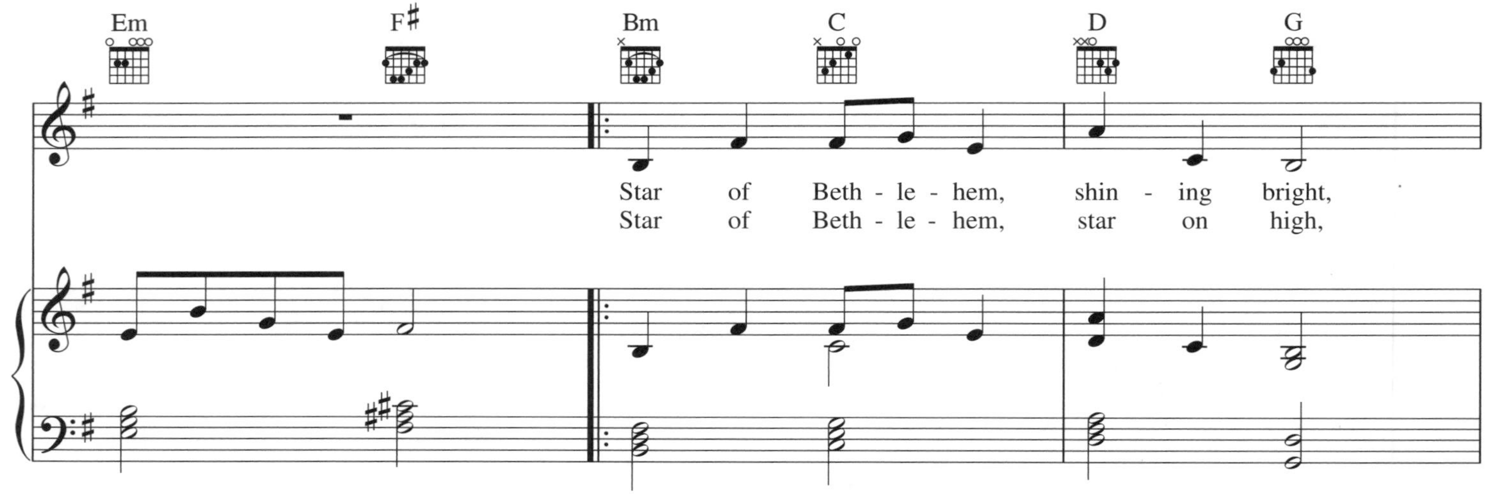

D G F#m7b5 Em D C B Em
4fr
dis - tant glo - ry fill us with hope this Christ - mas night.
light from heav - en en - ter our hearts and make us fly.
Cmaj7 Bm7 C D Em Cmaj7 F#m7b5/A
4fr
Star of in - no - cence, star of good - ness, gaz - ing down since
Star of hap - pi - ness, star of won - der, you see ev - 'ry - thing
C D E Am Em/G Am7 G
time be - gan, you who've lived through end - less ag - es,
from a - far. Cast your eye up - on the fu - ture,
C G/B Am G F# Bm C
view with love the age of man. Star of beau - ty,
make us wis - er than we are. Star of gen - tle - ness,

D
G
D/C
F♯m7♭5
B
4fr
hear our plea,
hear our plea,
whis - per your wis - dom ten - der - ly.
Em
Am
Dm7
G7
C
1
E7/B
Am
E7/G♯
Am
Star of Beth - le - hem, set us free,
make us a world we
Em/B
B7
Em
2
F♯m7♭5/A
Em/G
F♯m7♭5
Em
long to see.
make us a world we
F♯m7♭5/B
2fr
B7
Em
long to see.

Thank You Very Much

from SCROOGE

Words and Music by
Leslie Bricusse

Em7-5 Gm7/A A7 Dm Bbm/Db (Add A) Bbm/Db F/C F#o/C
done for us to - day
And there - fore I would
Gm7/C C7 F7 Cm/G Ab7 F7/A Ab7 Cm/G Ab/Gb F7 Cm7 F7
sim - ply like to say:
Refrain
Bb F9sus Bb Bb D7
1. Thank you ver - y much, Thank you ver - y much, That's the nic - est thing that
2. Thank you ver - y much, Thank you ver - y much, That's the nic - est thing that
3. Thank you ver - y much, Thank you ver - y much, That's the nic - est thing that
4. Thank you ver - y much, Thank you ver - y much, That's the nic - est thing that
mp
Gm C7 F7 Eb/G (Add F) Abm6 F7/A Cm Cm-5 Cm (Add D) Fm7/C F7
an-y-one's ev - er done for me I may sound dou - ble Dutch But
an-y-one's ev - er done for me It sounds a bit bi - zarre But
an-y-one's ev - er done for me It is - n't ev - 'ry day Good
an-y-one's ev - er done for me The fu - ture looks al - right In

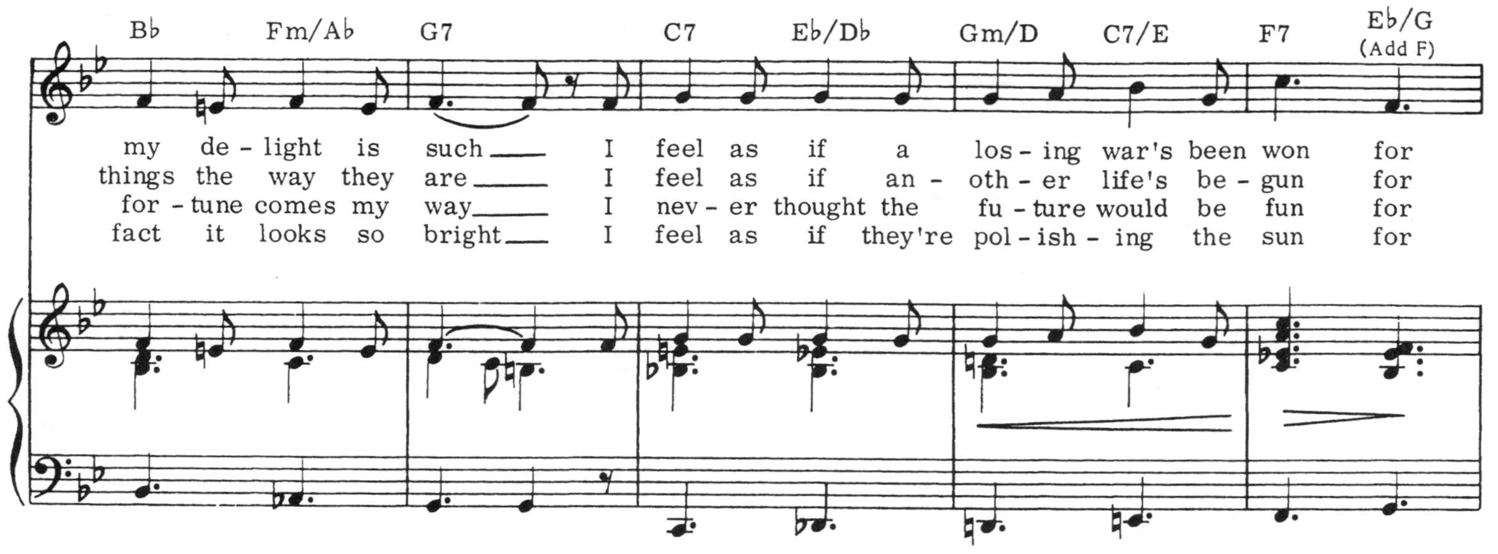

Bb Fm/Ab G7 C7 Eb/Db Gm/D C7/E F7 Eb/G (Add F)
my de - light is such I feel as if a los - ing war's been won for
things the way they are I feel as if an - oth - er life's be - gun for
for - tune comes my way I nev - er thought the fu - ture would be fun for
fact it looks so bright I feel as if they're pol - ish - ing the sun for

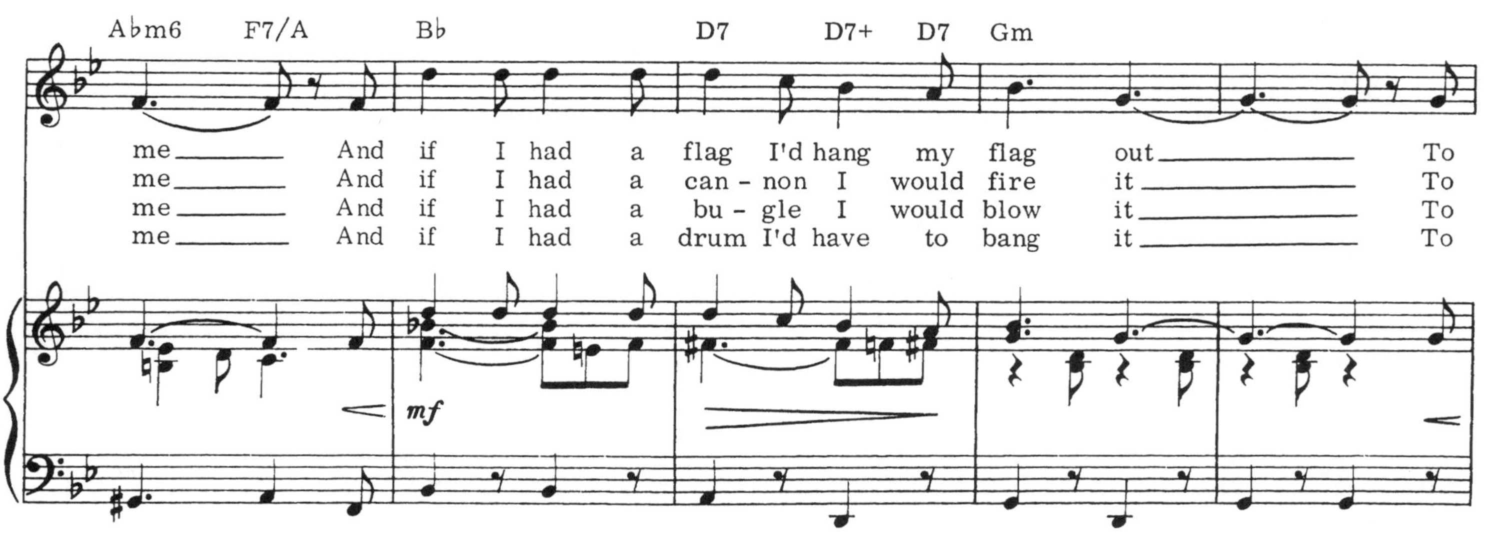

Abm6 F7/A Bb D7 D7+ D7 Gm
me And if I had a flag I'd hang my flag out To
me And if I had a can - non I would fire it To
me And if I had a bu - gle I would blow it To
me And if I had a drum I'd have to bang it To
mf

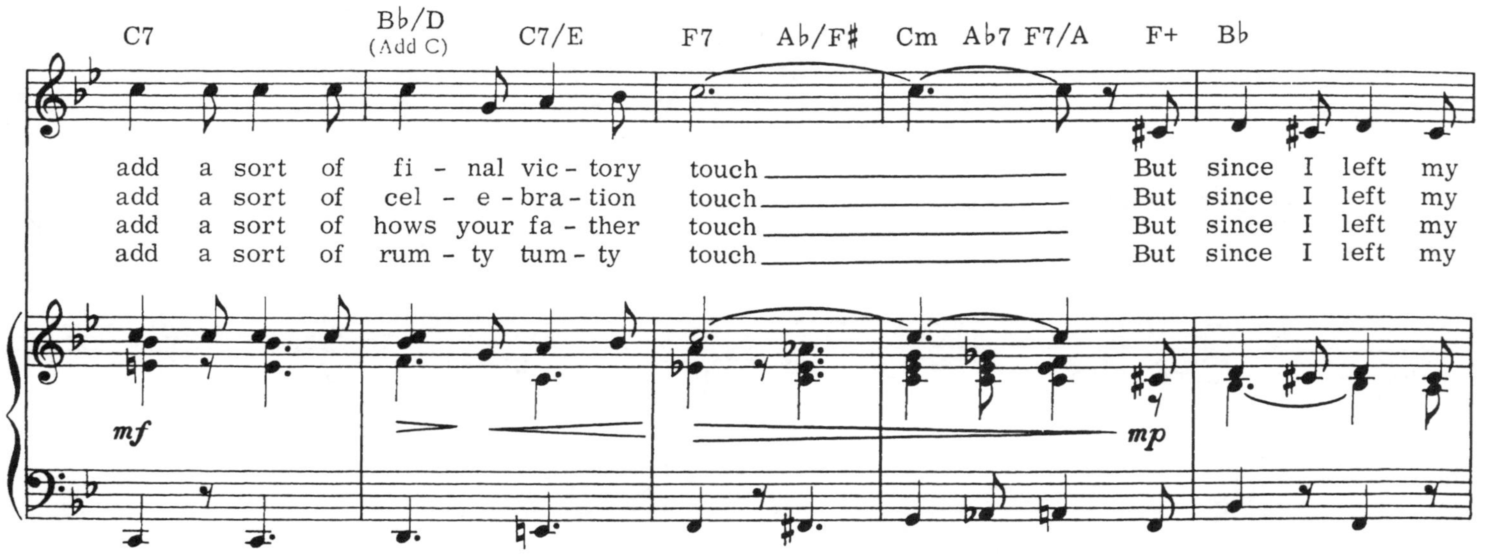

C7 Bb/D (Add C) C7/E F7 Ab/F# Cm Ab7 F7/A F+ Bb
add a sort of fi - nal vic - tory touch But since I left my
add a sort of cel - e - bra - tion touch But since I left my
add a sort of hows your fa - ther touch But since I left my
add a sort of rum - ty tum - ty touch But since I left my
mf
mp

Bb7 Eb D7sus D7 Gm Ebm/Gb Bb/F G7 C9 F7
flag at home I'll sim - ply have to say: Thank you ver - y, ver - y, ver - y
can - non at home I'll sim - ply have to say: Thank you ver - y, ver - y, ver - y
bu - gle at home I'll sim - ply have to say: Thank you ver - y, ver - y, ver - y
drum-mer at home I'll sim - ply have to say: Thank you ver - y, ver - y, ver - y
mf
1. 2. 3.
Bb Fm6/Ab Gm Ebm6/Gb Bb/F G/F Db/F F7
much.
much.
much.
much.
f mp cresc. poco a poco mf
4.
Gm Ebm/Gb Bb/F Bbm/F G7 C9 F7
Thank you ver - y ver - y ver - y
mf
Bb Gb/E Bb/F Gb/E Bb/F F7-5/Cb Bb
much!
f ff sfz

This Christmas

Words and Music by
Donny Hathaway and Nadine McKinnor

E♭maj7 Dm7 C13sus
3fr 8fr
Fmaj7
Dm9
3fr
this Christ - mas. And as we trim the tree, how much fun it's gon - na be to -
this Christ - mas. And as I look a - round your eyes out shine the town; they
E♭maj9
E♭maj7 Dm7 C13sus
3fr 8fr
Am7
geth - er this Christ - mas.
do, this Christ - mas. The fi - re - side is blaz - ing bright.
Solo ends
D9
4fr
Gm7
C7sus
We're car - ol - in' through the night and this
F
B7♯11
B♭maj7
E♭9
Am7
Dm7
Christ-mas will be a ver - y spe - cial Christ - mas for

Bm7b5
B7#11
1-3
Bbmaj7 Ebmaj7 Am Dm Abmaj9 Bbmaj7 Ebmaj7 F(add2)
me.
Bbmaj7 Ebmaj7 Am Dm Abmaj9 Bbmaj7 Ebmaj7 F(add2)
4
Bbmaj7 Ebmaj7 Am Dm Abmaj9 Bbmaj7 Ebmaj7 F(add2)
Mer - ry Christ - mas.
Bbmaj7 Ebmaj7 Am Dm Abmaj9 Bbmaj7 Ebmaj7 F(add2)
Shake your hand, shake your hand

B♭maj7
E♭maj7
Am
Dm
A♭maj9
B♭maj7
E♭maj7
F(add2)
now.
Wish your broth - er mer - ry Christ - mas
all o - ver the land
now.
Repeat and Fade
Optional Ending
Lead vocal ad lib.

We Need a Little Christmas

from MAME

Music and Lyric by
Jerry Herman

Am Am7 D7 Am7
stock - ing, I may be rush - ing
fruit - cake; it's time we hung some
Am7♭5 D7
things, but deck the halls a - gain
tin - sel on that ev - er - green
Dm6 E7 Am6 E7
now. For we
bough. For I've
For we
Am D7 G Gmaj7 G6 G+ G
3fr
need a lit - tle Christ - mas, right this ver - y min - ute,
grown a lit - tle lean - er, grown a lit - tle cold - er,
need a lit - tle mu - sic, need a lit - tle laugh - ter,

Am D7 G Gmaj7 G6 G7
can - dles in the win - dow, car - ols at the spin - et. Yes, we
grown a lit - tle sad - der, grown a lit - tle old - er. And I
need a lit - tle sing - ing ring - ing through the raft - er. And we
C D7 G Gmaj7 G6
To Coda
need a lit - tle Christ - mas, right this ver - y min - ute, it
need a lit - tle an - gel, sit - ting on my shoul - der, I
need a lit - tle snap - py "hap - py ev - er af - ter," we
1 A7 D7
has - n't snowed a sin - gle flur - ry, but San - ta, dear, we're in a hur - ry. So
2 Am
need a lit - tle
D9 D7 G
4fr
D.S. al Coda
Christ - mas now!
CODA
Am D9 D7 G
need a lit - tle Christ - mas now!

The Twelve Days of Christmas

Traditional English Carol

F F/A C7 C7/E F
5. On the fifth day of Christ - mas, my true love gave to me
F/A A♭°7 C7/G C7 F F/A Gm
five gold - en rings, four call - ing birds, three French hens,
C7 C7/E F F/A B♭ F/C C7 F B♭/F F
two tur - tle doves, and a par - tridge in a pear tree.
Fine
F F/A C7 C7/E F
Repeat as needed
C7
6. On the sixth day of Christ - mas, my true love gave to me six geese a - lay - ing,
7. On the sev - enth day of Christ - mas, my true love gave to me sev - en swans a - swim - ming,
8. On the eighth day of Christ - mas, my true love gave to me eight maids a - milk - ing,
9. On the ninth day of Christ - mas, my true love gave to me nine la - dies danc - ing,
10. On the tenth day of Christ - mas, my true love gave to me ten lords a - leap - ing,
11. On the 'lev - enth day of Christ - mas, my true love gave to me 'lev - en pip - ers pip - ing,
12. On the twelfth day of Christ - mas, my true love gave to me twelve drum - mers drum - ming,
D.S. for Verses 7-12;
Last time, D.S. al Fine
F A♭°7 C7/G C7
five gold - en rings,

Up on the Housetop

Words and Music by
B.R. Hanby

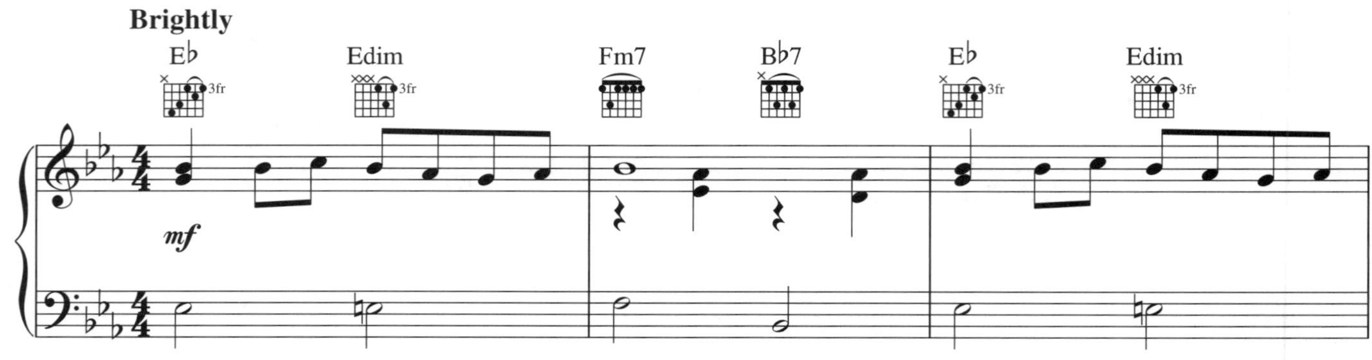

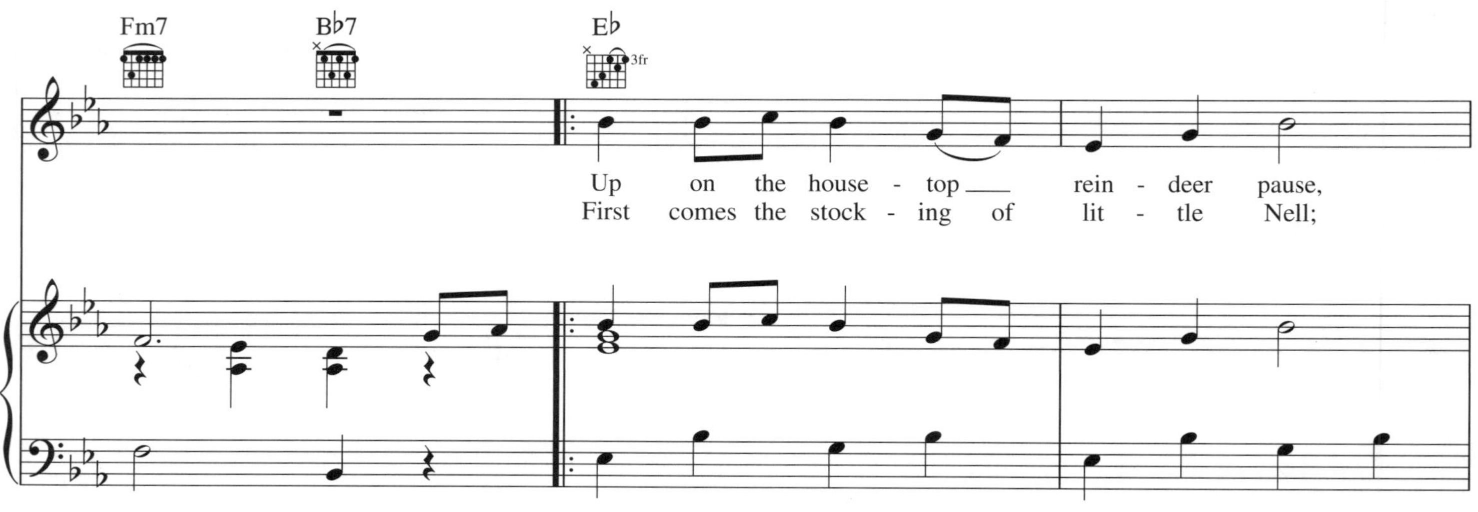

Ab
Eb/G
Bb7
Eb
lots of toys, All for the lit - tle ones, Christ - mas joys.
laughs and cries, One that will o - pen and shut her eyes.
Ab
Eb
Bb7
Ho, ho, ho! Who would - n't go! Ho, ho, ho!
Eb
Eb/Db
Ab/C
Eb/Bb
Ab
Who would - n't go! Up on the house - top, click, click, click,
Eb
Eb/G
Bb7
Eb
Down through the chim - ney with good Saint Nick.
3fr
4fr
6fr
3

We Wish You a Merry Christmas

Traditional English Folksong

F C/E Dm C Am F B♭ Gm C
tid - ings for Christ - mas and a hap - py New
F F B♭ D7/A
Year. Now bring us some fig - gy pud - ding, now
all love fig - gy pud - ding, we
won't go un - til we get some, we
G C A/C♯
bring us some fig - gy pud - ding, now bring us some fig - gy
all love fig - gy pud - ding, we all love fig - gy
won't go un - til we get some, we won't go un - til we
Dm F/A B♭ Gm C
1.2.
F
3.
F
D.C. al Fine
pud - ding and bring some out here. We here.
pud - ding, so bring some out here. We
get some, so bring some out

What Child Is This?

Words by William C. Dix

16th Century English Melody

2. Why lies He in such mean estate where ox and ass are feeding?
Good Christian, fear; for sinners here the silent Word is pleading.
Nails, spear, shall pierce Him through, the Cross be borne for me, for you.
Hail, hail, the Word made flesh, the Babe, the Son of Mary!

3. So bring Him incense, gold, and myrrh; come peasant, king to own Him.
The King of kings, salvation brings; let loving hearts enthrone Him.
Raise, raise the song on high; the Virgin sings her lullaby.
Joy, joy, for Christ is born, the Babe, the Son of Mary!

When Christmas Comes to Town

from Warner Bros. Pictures' THE POLAR EXPRESS

Words and Music by
Glen Ballard and Alan Silvestri

E♭sus E♭ Fm7 B♭/D
find me Christ - mas Eve. I guess that San - ta's bus - y 'cause he's
E♭ E♭/G A♭ E♭/G Fm7 B♭7sus
nev - er come a - round. I think of him when Christ - mas comes to
E♭ E♭sus E♭ E♭sus E♭ E♭sus E♭
town. The best time of the year when
mp
E♭sus E♭ E♭sus E♭ E♭sus E♭
ev - 'ry - one comes home; with all this Christ - mas cheer, it's hard to be a - lone.

Fm7
Bb/D
Eb
Eb/G
Ab
Eb/G
Put - ting up the Christ - mas tree with friends who come a - round, it's
Fm7
Fm7/Bb
Ebsus
Eb
so much fun when Christ - mas comes to town.
cresc.
Cb
Db/Cb
Bbm7
Ebm
Pres - ents for the chil - dren wrapped in red and green;
mf
Cb
Db/Cb
Bbm7
Ebm
all the things I've heard a - bout but nev - er real - ly seen.

Fm7♭5
Fm7♭5/E♭
B♭7/D
E♭m
E♭m/D
E♭m/D♭
4fr
6fr
No one will be sleep - ing on the night of Christ - mas Eve, __ hop - ing
F♯m7
B7
Fm7
B♭7sus
B♭7
E♭
E♭sus
E♭
3fr
6fr
3fr
San - ta's on his way.
mp
E♭sus
E♭
E♭sus
E♭
E♭sus
E♭
Fm7
Fm7/E♭
B♭/D
E♭
E♭/G
A♭
E♭/G
Fm7
Fm7/B♭
4fr

E♭sus
6fr
E♭
3fr
C♭
D♭/C♭
Pres - ents for the chil - dren
mf
B♭m7
E♭m
6fr
C♭
D♭/C♭
wrapped in red and green; all the things I've heard a - bout but
B♭m7
E♭m
6fr
Fm7♭5
Fm7♭5/E♭
4fr
B♭7/D
nev - er real - ly seen. No one will be sleep - ing on the
E♭m
6fr
E♭m/D
E♭m/D♭
F♯m7
B7
Fm7
B♭7sus
B♭7
night of Christ-mas Eve, hop - ing San - ta's on his way. When

E♭ E♭sus E♭ E♭sus E♭ E♭sus E♭
San-ta's sleigh bells ring, I lis-ten all a-round. The her-ald an-gels sing, I
mp
E♭sus E♭ Fm7 B♭/D
nev-er hear a sound. And all the dreams of chil-dren, once
E♭ E♭/G A♭ E♭/G Fm7 Fm7/B♭ Bdim7
lost, will now be found. That's all I want when Christ-mas comes to
Cm F9 Fm7 Fm7/B♭
town. That's all I want when Christ-mas comes

E♭
E♭sus
E♭
E♭sus
E♭
3fr
6fr
3fr
6fr
3fr
to town.
E♭sus
E♭
E♭sus
E♭
E♭sus
E♭
E♭sus
E♭
E♭sus
E♭
E♭sus
E♭
E♭sus
E♭
E♭sus
E♭
E♭sus
E♭
E♭sus
E♭
p

Where's the Line to See Jesus?

Words and Music by
Steve Haupt and Chris Loesch

E(add2)
C♯m
4fr
E(add2)
Chil-dren wait-ing for San - ta with ex-cite-ment and
C♯m
4fr
F♯m
B
glee. A lit-tle boy tugged my sweat-er,
F♯m
B
E
3
looked up and asked me, "Where's the line to see
mf
E+
3
Je - sus? Is He here at the store?

C♯m/E
4fr
Bm/E
E
F♯m7
If Christ-mas - time is His birth - day,
why don't we see Him
B7
E
more?
Where's the line to see Je - sus?
3
E+
C♯m/E
4fr
He was born for me.
San - ta Claus brought me
Bm/E
E7
F♯m7
B7
To Coda
E
pres - ents,
but Christ gave His life for me."

C♯m
4fr
E
C♯m
4fr
E(add2)
C♯m
4fr
E(add2)
As I stood in a - maze - ment at this mes - sage pro -
C♯m
4fr
F♯m
B
found, I looked down to thank him;
F♯m
B
E(add2)
he was no - where a - round. The lit - tle boy at the

C♯m
E(add2)
B/D♯
C♯m
4fr
mall might as well have had wings.
F♯m
B
F♯m
As the tears filled my eyes, thought I heard him
B
D.S. al Coda
sing,
CODA
E
Amaj7
B/A
me." In the blink of an eye, at the
G♯m7
C♯m
F♯m7
B
E
sound of His trump, we'll all stand in line at His throne. Ev-'ry
3

Amaj7
B/A
G♯m7
4fr
C♯m
4fr
F♯m7
knee shall bow down, ev-'ry tongue will con-fess that Je - sus Christ is
B
C
C7
F
Lord.
Where's the line to see
rall.
f a tempo
F+
Je - sus?
Is He here at the store?
3
Dm/F
Cm/F
3fr
F7
Gm7
If Christ-mas-time is His birth-day,
why don't we see Him

C7
F
more?
Where's the line to see Je - sus?
3
F+
Dm/F
He was born for me.
San - ta Claus brought me
Cm/F
F7
Gm7
C7
F
3fr
pres - ents,
but Christ gave His life for me.
rall.
mf a tempo
Dm
F(add2)
Dm
F(add2)
rit.

Wonderful Christmastime

Words and Music by
Paul McCartney

Cm7 Cm7/F Dm7 Gm9 E♭ A♭9 1 B♭
Sim - ply hav - ing a won - der - ful Christ - mas - time.
2, 3 B♭ Gm Cm7
time. The choir of chil - dren
F7 B♭ Gm Cm7
sing their song. 2nd time: (They prac - tised all year
To Coda
F7 B♭
long.) Ding dong, ding dong, ding

E♭
3fr
Cm7
3fr
dong, ding. Ooh, ooh.
E♭/B♭
6fr
E♭
3fr
B♭/D
Do do do
do do do do.
B♭
B♭maj7
B♭
Gm/B♭
B♭
F/B♭
B♭

Cm7
Cm7/F
Dm7
Gm9
E♭
A♭9
We're sim - ply hav - ing a won - der - ful Christ - mas -
B♭
Cm7
Cm7/F
Dm7
Gm9
E♭
A♭9
time. Sim - ply hav - ing a won - der - ful Christ - mas -
B♭
D.S. al Coda
(take 2nd ending)
time.
CODA
B♭
E♭/B♭
B♭
E♭/B♭
B♭
Ding dong, ding dong, ding
E♭/B♭
B♭
E♭/B♭
B♭
E♭/B♭
B♭
F7
dong, ding dong, ding dong, ding dong, dong

B♭
B♭maj7
dong, dong, dong. The par - ty's on,
B♭
Gm/B♭
B♭
B♭maj9
5fr
the spir - it's up, we're here to - night
B♭
and that's e - nough.
Cm7
3fr
Cm7/F
8fr
Dm7
Gm9
3fr
E♭
3fr
A♭9
4fr
B♭
Repeat and Fade
Sim - ply hav - ing a won - der - ful Christ - mas - time. We're
sim - ply hav - ing a won - der - ful Christ - mas - time.